Hybrid Organizations

HYBRID
ORGANIZATIONS

New Business Models for Environmental Leadership

Brewster Boyd, Nina Henning, Emily Reyna, Daniel E. Wang, and Matthew D. Welch

With a Foreword by Andrew Hoffman

Greenleaf
PUBLISHING

Published by Greenleaf Publishing Limited
Aizlewood's Mill
Nursery Street
Sheffield S3 8GG
UK
www.greenleaf-publishing.com

Printed in Great Britain on acid-free paper by CPI Antony Rowe, Chippenham, Wiltshire

FSC
Mixed Sources
Product group from well-managed
forests and other controlled sources
Cert no. SGS-COC-2953
www.fsc.org
© 1996 Forest Stewardship Council

Cover by LaliAbril.com

British Library Cataloguing in Publication Data:

   Hybrid organizations : new business models for
     environmental leadership.
     1. Industrial management--Environmental aspects.
     2. Industrial management--Environmental aspects--Case
     studies.
     I. Boyd, Brewster.
     658.4'08–dc22

     ISBN-13: 9781906093273

Contents

Foreword vii
  Andrew J. Hoffman, Holcim (U.S.) Professor of Sustainable Enterprise,
  University of Michigan

Acknowledgments xii

Introduction 1

  1 Why hybrid organizations? 5

  2 The hybrid landscape 11

  3 Uncovering the layers 18

  4 Hybrid trends and lessons 25

  5 Case study
    SUN OVENS International — patient dealmaker 37

  6 Case study
    Guayakí — creating an entirely new value chain 63

  7 Case study
    Eden Foods — lasting leadership and the risks of succession 90

  8 Case study
    Maggie's Organics — connecting producers and consumers
    to the cause 106

9 Case study
PAX Scientific — learning to run 128

10 Business lessons for hybrid organizations 144

11 Reflecting back, looking forward 150

References 154

Appendix: List of hybrid organizations completing survey 160

About the authors 163

Index 165

Foreword

Andrew J. Hoffman
Holcim (U.S.) Professor of Sustainable Enterprise, University of Michigan

The book you are holding is a glimpse into the future. The companies it describes are pioneers, the first-movers in market shifts that will eventually become mainstream. These "hybrid organizations" — or what others call "values-driven" or "mission-driven" organizations — operate in the blurry space between the for-profit and nonprofit worlds. Indeed, we see many companies today — large and small — touting social and environmental missions much like a nonprofit organization. And, conversely, we see many nonprofits developing business models much like that of a for-profit business (Ten Thousand Villages, for example, is a volunteer-run, fair trade 501(c)(3) nonprofit retail store providing income to artisans from more than 30 countries). The companies described in this book fall into the first category but are stretching those boundaries even further. They are redefining their supply chains, their sources of capital, their very purpose for being; and in the process they are changing the market for others.

If you don't believe this, take a look at what just happened in the area of environmentally sensitive cleaning products. For more than 20 years, a hybrid organization named Seventh Generation had created a niche for itself, "becoming the world's most trusted brand of authentic, safe, and environmentally-responsible products for a healthy home." In the process, the company enjoyed the financial benefits of being the dominant player in a small but increasingly lucrative market. But today, that niche is going mainstream. In 2008, Oakland, California-based Clorox added a series of natural, biodegradable household cleaners called Green Works to its $4.8 billion family of cleaning and household products. Think about it: the company that has become synonymous with the most toxic substance that the average homeowner will ever bring into their home — bleach — is now expanding into the green cleaners space. Seventh Generation was the first-mover, saw the market potential, educated and cultivated its consumers, developed the products, and reaped the benefits. But now that the market is materializing, the business strategy of others in the consumer goods industry is to move into the space. This is just one anecdote that describes what these hybrid organizations can do to the market.

So who are these hybrid organizations? What makes them different? How do they operate? What is this glimpse into the future that they offer? These are the questions that this book answers. The first thing that struck me when reading the early drafts of this research is that many of these companies believe that they are unique, that there are few others doing what they do. But the reality is that there is a growing number of companies breaking this new ground, each in their own way. In this book, you will read about the best practices of 47 companies whose central mission is to use capitalism to solve the world's environmental and social problems. For example, you will read about Guayakí, a company that sells organic, rainforest-grown, fair trade yerba mate but is really devoted to delivering "unique and beneficial products that enhance personal health and well being" and "create economic models that drive reforestation while employing a living wage" for the benefit of farmers and indigenous communities. Or you will read about SUN OVENS, a company formed to:

> . . . develop and implement comprehensive solar cooking programs that will radically decrease the developing world's dependence on fuel wood and dung as the primary cooking fuels while benefiting the environment, raising the standard of living and improving the health of the poor worldwide.

And PAX Scientific, a company dedicated to applying "nature's core design principles to engineer energy-efficient products that enhance and sustain life on Earth" by using biomimicry to improve fluid-handling equipment.

The social and environmental missions that these companies espouse are not just some tag line or marketing pitch. They really mean it. How do we know that? Their business models don't just reflect their mission; they embody it. For example, these companies develop deep relationships with suppliers, producers, and customers that go much farther than the contemporary business model. As the authors so aptly state, "Hybrid organizations operate in clear contrast to the cliché, 'it isn't personal, it's business.'" For example, Maggie's Organics, the oldest organic apparel company in the United States has created sewing co-operatives in Nicaragua to source its cotton fabrics from self-sustaining collaboratives. Similarly, Guayakí pays its farmers above-market "living wages" and devotes significant time and resources to training them in sustainable farming techniques. Clearly, there are easier and cheaper ways to obtain their raw materials and resources, but these companies have chosen to do business with their mission front and center.

These are just small glimpses of what is inside this book. There is much more to explain about the best practices of what these companies do and why. But one thing that rings loud and clear — this is not a mere passing fad. These companies show a tenacity and patience that make clear that they are not in it for a quick buck. They are in it for the long haul. It is said that "a man will do so much for a buck, more for another man, but he will die for a cause." Well, these companies are committed to a cause that will take one or more generations to realize and they will see it through. SUN OVENS, for example, has been skirting on the edge of bankruptcy for its entire existence — what President Paul Munsen describes as a balance sheet that is "more than bankrupt" — but is not wavering. Guayakí CEO Chris Mann acknowledges that his company could expand far faster if it was willing to compromise its mission and source mate in ways that do not promote protection of the Atlantic Rainforest. But that is not an option for a hybrid organization. And, as a result of such commitment, these companies can be counted on to — in the words of one of Clif Bar's Five Aspirations — "grow slower, grow better and stick around longer." And, in so doing, they will alter the markets in which they operate.

Eden Foods, for example, has been working to "provide the highest quality organic foods for the benefit of our customers" since 1968. The company's longevity has enabled it to play a key role in shaping the growth of the organic food market. Looking to the future, PAX Scientific is poised to make the leap to commercial success in the "clean tech" market after ten years of careful growth and development. As the authors explain, "PAX has learned to move from a 'crawl' to a 'walk' . . . [and has now] made a deliberate decision to accelerate the business to a 'run.'"

And this is when it gets fun. Capitalism really is being used to promote social and environmental missions.

But don't think that these companies will now rest on their laurels. Successful companies become acquisition targets for other companies. While some yield to the appeal of a buy-out offer — Ben & Jerry's was acquired by Unilever in 2000, Stonyfield Farm was acquired by the Danone Group in 2003, Burt's Bees was acquired by Clorox in 2008 — others resist the financial enticement to remain true to their ultimate mission, values, and purpose. Chris Mann, echoing the sentiments of other hybrid business owners, has struggled with the decision to bring on partner financing. The problem he says is that "[venture capitalists] want control. It would be difficult to maintain our mission if we only have 30% or 40% control."

In the end, what you should glean from the brief descriptions above and the deeper analysis within these pages is that the business models that hybrid organizations are developing are models that are sustainable in the long term because they are developed carefully over the short term. And this is the kind of commitment and growth plan that any analyst on Wall Street would like to see. It is what high-quality companies do. They develop:

- A long-term plan that is based on a solid product or service that a growing market will support

- Close relationships with suppliers that will assure continued resources for maintaining that market

- Committed leaders guided by a clear vision that will sustain through generations

This is not unlike what admired companies like Johnson & Johnson, DuPont, and others have done to stay successful for long-term growth. And it is the kind of company that today's best and brightest young people are looking for when they enter the workforce.

I can tell you that, as a university professor looking back over the past 20 years, today's students are mission-driven to an extent unheard of a generation ago. A company with a strong social and environmental mission is what they want. And some companies are beginning to notice. Jeffrey Immelt, CEO of GE, has publicly stated that his company's Ecomagination program has improved recruiting efforts immensely. Patagonia, with its strong environmental and social mission, boasts that for every opening it receives thousands of applications. As the companies in this book show, this isn't something you can fake. And to develop a mission-driven culture you need to understand what these hybrid organizations already know, even if they don't fully admit it — real values and mission can only be developed slowly, over the long term to be truly lasting and credible. Bená Burda, founder and President of Maggie's Organics, the oldest organic apparel company in the U.S., humbly states: "I am not a fair trade person, and I'm not socially responsible. This is simply the way we choose to do business and we wouldn't do it any other way." But pay heed, while they may not question what they are doing, they are defining the norms for the market to come. In short, the way they do business today provides a glimpse into how business will be done tomorrow.

Andrew J. Hoffman
Holcim (U.S.) Professor of Sustainable Enterprise
The University of Michigan
Ann Arbor, Michigan
November 2008

Acknowledgments

Many groups and individuals were involved in the research and writing of this book. First, we would like to thank all 47 of the hybrid organizations that participated in our survey. We know that time is a scarce resource, and we hope that this book gives them a return that is well worth the time they invested in our project.

We would also like to thank those we spoke with at our case study companies for allowing us entry into their hybrid organizations and for sharing some of the subtle challenges and opportunities that they face:

- Michael Potter, Sue Becker, Jay Hughes, Jon Solomon, and Bill Swaney at Eden Foods

- Chris Mann and Richard Bruehl at Guayakí

- Bená Burda and Doug Wilson at Maggie's Organics

- Jay Harman, Francesca Bertone, Laura Bertone, and Kasey Arnold-Ince at PAX Scientific

- Paul Munsen at SUN OVENS

Their aid and information shaped a large part of our analysis.

In addition, we express gratitude to the University of Michigan's School of Natural Resources and Environment, Ross School of Business, and Erb Institute for Global Sustainable Enterprise for providing numerous resources essential for this project to proceed. In particular, we would like to thank Andy Hoffman, our faculty advisor, for his continued belief in our work, for providing personal and professional support, and for offering critical and ever-insightful appraisals of our efforts. We are grateful to Kelly Janiga at the William Davidson Institute, without whose sponsorship our project would never have left the ground. We also thank John Branch, our case writing advisor, for all of his advice into the process and structure of illustrative case writing. Our sincere appreciation goes to Kelly Sission for editing the early incarnations of this book. We would also like to thank the entire staff at Greenleaf Publishing for providing the opportunity to communicate the ideas and innovations of hybrid organizations to a broad audience through this publication.

Last and certainly not least, we are incredibly grateful to our friends and, more importantly, our families, for their continued patience and support during the 18-month process of researching and writing this book.

Introduction

This book explores trends and lessons learned from hybrid organizations pursuing environmental sustainability missions. It hypothesizes that hybrid organizations — defined here as entities that are both market-oriented and mission-centered — can contribute positively to some of humanity's most pressing challenges by executing on business models that have values-based missions baked in. These organizations, which place equal emphasis on their common-good mission and financial performance, blur the distinction between nonprofit and for-profit entities.

This book has six sections. The first section (Chapter 1) includes key definitions to establish the scope of the project, including explicit definitions for hybrid organizations, environmental sustainability missions, as well as specific criteria to narrow the field to a meaningful list of hybrid organizations. The second section (Chapter 2) represents an extensive review of the existing literature on models that blend traditional nonprofit and traditional for-profit characteristics. Building on prior work conducted by researchers on corporate social responsibility, sustainable entrepreneurship, and social enterprise, the existing research identifies a specific gap in the literature: little is known about the contributions of privately held, for-profit businesses with environmental sustainability missions. The third section (Chapter 3) describes the investigation methodology, specifically stating the procedures and rationale used to identify the hybrid organizations, to develop and administer the survey, and to select the five organizations on which to conduct in-depth case studies.

The fourth section (Chapter 4) synthesizes the survey data from 47 hybrid organizations, investigating their business models and strategies, finances, organizational structures, processes, metrics, and innovations. The organizations represent a cross-section of size, age, industry, and geography, although the sample set is biased towards young, small, U.S.-based hybrids. The fifth section (Chapters 5–9) details five best-in-class company case studies. Each case describes a company's distinct approach to balancing environmental and profit goals. Finally, the sixth section (Chapters 10 and 11) discusses lessons learned and future research directions for hybrid organizations.

The survey data reveal a mix of expected and surprising trends. For example, in relation to the integration of business practices that enable companies to meet both mission and market goals, hybrid organizations employ innovative products in niche markets, leverage patient capital to meet non-financial objectives, and encourage shared authority rather than top-down leadership styles. And, although respondents show varying levels of profitability, they maintain consistently high levels of environmental sustainability integration throughout their firms. Table 1 summarizes key trends by organizational characteristic.

TABLE 1 Key trends for hybrid organizations

Organizational characteristic	Observed pattern for hybrid organizations
Business model and strategy	• 66% believe they do something completely different from competitors • Innovative product and environmental features are key sources of competitive advantage
Finance	• 50/50 split between positive and negative profit margins • 59% of hybrid funding comes from patient capital • Financing for hybrids can be both an advantage and disadvantage
Organization	• 75% are led by transformational or participative leaders • 83% have "fully integrated environmental sustainability"
Processes and metrics	• 55% track environmental metrics
Innovation	• 65% have "notable innovations" relating to product or service

These survey data set the stage for the five case studies, where several major practices can be gleaned:

- Implementing the mission in action

- Uncommonly close, personal relationships

- Patience

- Limits to growth rate

- Market premium products; rarely compete on price

The first practice, **implementing the mission in action**, refers to the fact that the mission is embedded in the business model and in all key decisions across organizational levels of best-in-class hybrids. The second practice, **uncommonly close, personal relationships**, highlights the deliberate personal connections to suppliers, producers, and customers that hybrids undertake; for hybrid organizations, business is clearly personal. The third practice is **patience**. Ambitious dual-minded missions across generations require patience for all stakeholders, both financial and non-financial. The fourth practice, **limits to growth rate**, identifies the challenge for hybrids to scale their business while balancing mission and profit goals. Not to be confused with limits to growth, this theme specifically derives from hybrids experiencing less than maximum speed of growth because of self-imposed mission constraints. The final practice, **market premium products; rarely compete on price**, is a reflection of hybrid organizations competing as quality market leaders in their industries. They develop new game strategies to build and establish themselves in novel market segments.

However, it is no single practice that sets apart hybrid organizations from traditional for-profit or nonprofit entities. Rather, it is the combination of these innovative practices that allows hybrids to meet their mission- and market-centric goals in an effective manner. Hybrid organizations utilize an integrated system of non-traditional business activities that allow them to bridge the gap between mission and finance.

In short, this research suggests that hybrid organizations offer a practical and feasible organizational model for contributing solutions to global environmental issues. Survey and case study data provide evidence of targeted, self-sustaining successes. While there may be limits to the speed of growth or scale of impact, particularly for place-based solutions, hybrid organizations can indeed be more effective and enduring than traditional organizations in meeting humanity's common challenges.

1
Why hybrid organizations?

FIGURE 1 Hybrid organization definition

See also page 18.

Hybrid organization

A market–oriented and common–good mission–centered organization. Hybrid organizations may exhibit the following characteristics:
- Non–financial performance valuation
- Privately held by connected, individual investors
- Sub–market rates of return
- Alternative capitalization

This book presents the results of an 18-month effort into researching companies that pursue the two-pronged goal of environmental sustainability and profitability. Such organizations are referred to here as **hybrid organizations** ("a market-oriented and common-good mission-centered organization; see Fig. 1). This book compiles the wisdom, trends, and lessons learned from the 47 hybrid organizations that provided valuable responses to survey questions about strategies, finances, organizational structure, leadership, processes, and innovations. Five of these companies allowed the research team to perform interviews with their organizations for the development of case studies.

The hypothesis for this research is that the inherent business model of hybrid organizations can contribute positively to environmental sustainability outcomes. The business model of this type of organization strives to have a positive impact on the environment, not just to minimize or reduce negative impact. Hybrids are different from traditional for-profit and nonprofit organizations because their primary motivation is to use business and market forces as tools to solve the world's largest challenges. This book highlights hybrid organizations that are effectively combining goals of financial viability and environmental stewardship.

Since minimal research has been done on this combination, the main aim of this book is to explore the trends, solutions, and lessons learned from hybrid organizations with specific environmental missions. Documentation and better understanding of these findings may facilitate value creation for other practitioners in this sector, as well as provoke discussion among researchers exploring high-impact organizations. Furthermore, understanding the struggles and successes of the hybrid organizations in this study will help future entrepreneurs combat environmental degradation in more effective ways.

Background — hybrid organizations defined

According the United Nations Millennium Development Goals, poverty, income and gender inequality, disease, and environmental degradation are among the most challenging problems facing the world today (Sachs 2005). Numerous approaches to solving these problems have been attempted by local and national governments, international organizations, regional nonprofit organizations, and for-profit businesses seeking to adhere to corporate social responsibility (CSR) standards. While no one company or organization is expected to solve the world's problems alone, some nonprofit and for-profit organizations endeavor to be valuable and significant contributors to larger solutions. However, the current approaches of both traditional nonprofits and for-profits have often proven ineffective in generating and continuing large-scale change.

A growing understanding exists in the nonprofit world that traditional funding sources will no longer be adequate to address such problems and that organizations cannot rely upon a continuous supply of donor funding for their operations (Alexander 2000; Draper 2005). The result is a need for a new emphasis on social enterprise models that provides some direction for solving this funding problem through earned income creation, though work in this field is in a nascent phase. Various challenges remain to be solved in this new area; for example: the tax classification of nonprofit social enterprises, potential mission drift among nonprofits undertaking earned income strategies, and achieving consensus regarding the appropriateness of nonprofit organizations in competitive business ventures (Billitteri 2007; Foster and Bradach 2005; Heritage and Orlebeke 2004). For all the important work being done by nonprofit organizations throughout the world, such effort has yielded limited success in achieving large-scale solutions.

Traditional businesses have fared even worse due to their reluctance to address development goals, primarily leaving social and environmental issues to government agencies and civil society. Though some people argue that the majority of the problems facing the world are the result of market failures, many businesses answer that it is not in their corporate mandate to attempt to address these problems. This situation is slowly changing, and many businesses now understand that it is in their best interest to deal with social and environmental issues (Beheiry *et al.* 2006; Hillman and Keim 2001; Swanson 1999). The growth of corporate philanthropy and sustainability departments within many large multinational corporations attests to this changing attitude among businesses. However, even with this new emphasis on social and environmental issues, the traditional business model often fails to adequately address the critical problems facing the world today.

Some propose that the optimal approach combines the best of nonprofit organizations and for-profit businesses. These hybrid models — which are variously referred to as Fourth Sector, Blended Value, For-Benefit, or B-Corporations — may hold promise for addressing the most troublesome challenges facing both the developed and developing worlds (Billitteri 2007; Emerson and Bonini 2003; Strom 2007).[1] While some research has been conducted on this type of organization, few comprehensive studies have been completed and little has been done to understand company best practices in this field (Alter 2004; Haugh 2005; Smallbone *et al.* 2001).

Kim Alter, Founder and Managing Director of Virtue Ventures, has conducted research on hybrid organizations. Her hybrid spectrum, repro-

---

1 See also "About B Corp"; www.bcorporation.net/about, accessed January 29, 2009.

duced in Figure 2, categorizes hybrids along a continuum according to their relative position between the traditional nonprofit and for-profit spaces. The Virtue Ventures website states:

> All hybrid organizations generate both social and economic value and are organized by degree of activity as it relates to: 1) motive, 2) accountability, and 3) use of income.[2]

Alter's model presents a taxonomy of four types of hybrid organizations. On the left side of the hybrid spectrum are those nonprofits whose business activities generate profits to fund their social mission and report back to their stakeholders. On the right side of the hybrid spectrum are for-profit companies that create social value, but are mainly driven by profits and are accountable to shareholders.

FIGURE 2 Alter's hybrid spectrum

Source: www.virtueventures.com/setypology/index.php?id=HYBRID_SPECTRUM&lm=0

Hybrid spectrum

Traditional nonprofit	Nonprofit with income–generating activities	Social enterprise	Socially responsible business	Corporation practicing social responsibility	Traditional for-profit

Mission motive · • Profit-making motive

Stakeholder accountability · • Shareholder accountability

Income reinvested in social programs · • Profit redistributed to shareholders
or operational costs

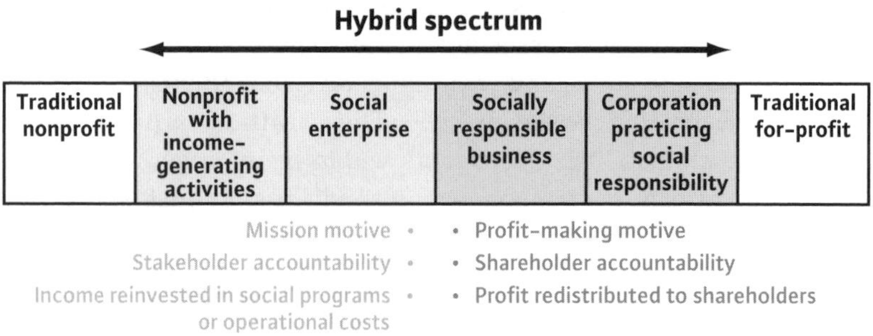

While Alter's model is useful in representing differences and trade-offs among hybrid organizations, we propose that the realm of hybrid organizations cannot be categorized along the single dimension that her model employs; rather, profit and mission motives are relatively independent organizational dimensions. Indeed, hybrid organizations exist that are highly driven by both profit and mission, and thus challenge the notion of trade-offs between mission and profit motives. We developed the illustration in Figure 3 to represent the blurring of boundaries between traditional nonprofit and for-profit organizations.

---

2 www.virtueventures.com/setypology/index.php?id=HYBRID_SPECTRUM&lm=0, accessed May 27, 2009.

FIGURE 3 Mission and profit dimensions of business models

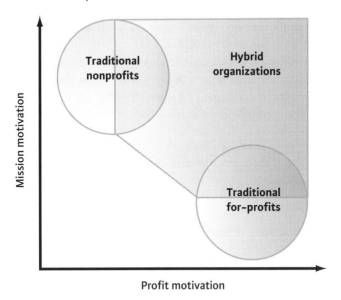

This book explores organizations motivated by both mission and profit. Such hybrid organizations not only blur the distinctions between the nonprofit and for-profit sectors but, through their emphasis on environmental, social, and financial value creation, they also provide another business model for addressing worldwide societal problems. For-profit hybrid organizations will not be held accountable solely to the legal fiduciary duty to their shareholders, and can thus gain the flexibility to be innovative in their approaches to these problems. At the same time, because these organizations depend on sufficient profitability to maintain existence and serve their missions, critics may contend that they are hampered by their dual motivations.

Scope

A hybrid organization is defined as a market-oriented, common-good mission-centered organization which operates in the blurred space between traditional for-profit and nonprofit enterprises. In reviewing industry and academic literature, we identified a gap in research on hybrid organizations that are, in particular, for-profit and privately owned. The goal of this book is to fill that gap, with a specific focus on companies with an environmental sustainability mission.

This book narrows criteria for environmental sustainability mission-driven companies to encompass those where either the direct business activity (products or services) or the most significant inputs, raw materials, or resources contribute to at least one of the following basic human needs:

- Clean air
- Clean energy
- Clean water
- Sustainable food or agricultural systems
- Sustainable housing

2
The hybrid landscape

While little has been written about for-profit hybrid organizations, a larger body of literature exists on corporate social responsibility, sustainable businesses, and nonprofit social enterprises. These fields provide the basis for hybrid organizations, but the focus has often been narrow or concentrated on a single aspect of the field.

Research into traditional businesses does not address organizations that go beyond corporate social responsibility. While some authors have shown that it is in businesses' best interest to deal with social and environmental issues (Beheiry *et al.* 2006; Hillman and Keim 2001; Reed and WRI 2001; Swanson 1999), they do not address organizations that make these their primary mission.

Recently, a good deal of literature has been written about social entrepreneurship, but a general focus on addressing social problems mostly ignores environmental issues. A new emphasis on sustainable entrepreneurship — the creation of businesses that have both social and environmental goals — has garnered much attention, but literature on the subject also falls short of offering a comprehensive understanding of hybrid organizations. Sustainable entrepreneurship research deals primarily with the formation of these enterprises, and the motivations behind them. In addition, some recent research has focused on nonprofit and business cooperation, but these projects fail to address hybrid organizations which bridge the two types of organizational motives. Overall, the literature on hybrid organizations remains lacking with regard to research specifically addressing hybrid organizations.

Corporate social responsibility

Corporate social responsibility is not a new concept, but recently it has received much research interest. Many writers have attempted to show that business is a force for change with regards to social and environmental issues, and can be a main driver to create a more just and sustainable world (Hart 2005; Prahalad 2005; Robinson 2004; SustainAbility 2007). This research has been both theoretical and empirical, with much focus on the effect of corporate social responsibility on the financial performance of an organization. The empirical evidence is mixed with regard to the relationship between social focus and financial success. Some suggest a trade-off between the two (Burke and Logsdon 1996; McGuire *et al.* 1988; McWilliams and Siegel 2000), while others do not conceptualize the relationship in such a straightforward manner.

Empirical and theoretical research has explored corporate social responsibility for almost 50 years. Early empirical researchers supported the idea that superior business practice equated to social responsibility (Davis 1960; Whetten *et al.* 2002; Wren 1979). More recently, some researchers have concurred, suggesting that businesses need to respond to social issues in order to be viable (Engen 2005; Johnson 2000), while others have seen it as simply good business sense (Dentchev 2004; Epstein and Roy 2003).

During these same decades, theoretical approaches have looked into more descriptive studies of corporate social responsibility. Much has been written about the importance of the attitudinal motivations of managers toward corporate social responsibility, trumping the financial factors involved (Bowman and Haire 1975; Déniz-Déniz and García-Falcón 2002; Marz *et al.* 2003; Quazi and O'Brien 2000; Rojšek 2001). Others have relied on case studies to understand corporate social responsibility (Weiser and Zadek 2000). Overall, this research has simply set the stage for further inquiry into the linkages between corporate social responsibility and financial performance.

While theoretical research into corporate social responsibility has suggested a positive relationship between businesses' response to social issues and financial performance (Carroll 1999; Wood 1991), the empirical evidence is mixed. Over the years, many different studies have attempted to show that corporate social responsibility is good for business. However, no clear consensus on this linkage has emerged. The results have run the gamut from a negative relationship between the two, to a neutral one, and finally to a positive relationship. Table 2 provides an overview of the findings of this relationship.

TABLE 2 Research on linkages between social and financial performance

For a more detailed example, see Salzmann *et al.* 2005

Relationship	Framework	Author(s)
Negative	Trade–off	Friedman (1962)
		Vance (1975)
	Managerial opportunism	Preston and O'Bannon (1997)
		Posner and Schmidt (1992)
		Alkhafaji (1989)
	Negative synergy	Preston and O'Bannon (1997)
Neutral	Supply and demand theory	McWilliams and Siegel (2000)
		Anderson and Frankle (1980)
		Aupperle *et al.* (1985)
		Freedman and Jaggi (1982)
Positive	Social impact	Cornell and Shapiro (1987)
		Pava and Krausz (1996)
		Preston and O'Bannon (1997)
	Available funds/slack resources	Waddock and Graves (1997)
		McGuire *et al.* (1988)
		Kraft and Hage (1990)
	Positive synergy	Waddock and Graves (1997)
		Stanwick and Stanwick (1998)
		Preston and O'Bannon (1997)
		Pava and Krausz (1996)

Although no agreement exists concerning the relationship between corporate social responsibility and financial performance, this research has been helpful in establishing a baseline understanding of hybrid organizations. This concept of corporate social responsibility represents a precursor to hybrid organizational theory, and understanding the parallels can illuminate the motivations and expectations of hybrid organization practitioners. However, the research falls short of clarifying what exactly a hybrid organization is and how it functions in the realm of business and nonprofit organizations. Furthermore, the research often leaves out any mention of environmental motivations and performance.

Sustainable entrepreneurship

Another topic receiving considerable research over the past few years is sustainable entrepreneurship. The focus of this research has been primarily based on the entrepreneurial aspects of businesses and individuals, and their use in improving environmental and social issues. While this research is exceptionally valuable to the understanding of hybrid organizations and their creation, once again the focus illuminates only a small part of what constitutes a hybrid.

Much of the research in this area starts with the traditional definition of entrepreneurship as value creation through innovation (Drucker 2006; Schumpeter 1989). Some simply view sustainable entrepreneurs as one category of entrepreneurs with little difference between them and traditional entrepreneurs (Dees 1998a). Others see values-based sustainable enterprises as a different breed requiring a unique perspective (Brown and NetLibrary Inc. 2005; Parrish 2005).

A great deal of recent research has been undertaken in the field of sustainable entrepreneurship (Abrahamsson 2007; Cohen and Winn 2005; Crals and Vereeck 2004; Keijzers 2002), and entrepreneurs in this field have been called by many different names (Emerson and Twersky 1996). The term **ecopreneur** dates back to the early 1990s. Labels such as **ecopreneuring** and **ecopreneurship** have shown up in the literature since this time (Bennett 1991; Blue 1990; Dixon and Clifford 2007; Schaper 2002, 2005). The term **green entrepreneur** has also been used to label practitioners in this field (Berle 1991). Finally, the label of **sustainability entrepreneurship** or **sustainopreneurship** has shown up in more recent research (Abrahamsson 2007; Gerlach 2003a,b; Hockerts 2003; Schaltegger 2000). However, regardless of the terminology, the commonality among entrepreneurs in this field is their use of traditional business skills and knowledge to accomplish social and environmental goals.

While the idea of sustainable entrepreneurship appears quite similar to hybrid organizations, the research is limited. The focus on sustainable entrepreneurship helps to understand the motivation of individual entrepreneurs and the formation of their companies. However, it does not assist in comprehending the ongoing operations of mature hybrids or their adaptation to changes as markets mature. The use of different terms to discuss sustainable enterprises and their practitioners confuses the issue still further. Additional research is needed in order to understand many of the issues facing hybrid organizations. Although the research into sustainable entrepreneurship can help understand the formation and players behind hybrid organizations, its focus is necessarily more narrow than the broader scope of hybrid organizations.

Social enterprise and business — nonprofit alliances

As noted above, many writers see for-profit businesses and nonprofit organizations as existing on a continuum, with pure businesses seeking only profit maximization on one end of the spectrum and values-based organizations working solely for environmental or social issues on the other end of the spectrum (Alter 2004; Conaty 2001; Peredo and McLean 2006). Social enterprises are often placed near the center of the spectrum, and are almost exclusively looked upon as nonprofit ventures. Alliances between nonprofits and businesses are simply viewed as linkages between two separate parts of the spectrum. While the research into nonprofit social enterprises is quite extensive, little emphasis is placed on for-profit businesses with similar goals and aspirations. Also, although the alliance between nonprofits and for-profits is beginning to receive more attention, almost no attention is given to organizations that fully encompass both ends of the spectrum in a single enterprise.

Much of the research into social enterprises focuses solely on non-profit organizations (Dees 1998b; Dees *et al.* 2004; Emerson and Twersky 1996; Hall 2005). Some state that social enterprises can be formed only through nonprofit organizations (Taylor *et al.* 2000) or view social entrepreneurship simply as good business practice within nonprofits (Reis and Clohesy 2001). Others question whether social enterprises are good for nonprofit organizations or addressing social issues (Casselman 2007; Foster and Bradach 2005). While the majority of the research on social enterprise focuses solely on the nonprofit realm, comprehension of this organizational form still proves advantageous in understanding for-profit hybrid models.

The research on social entrepreneurship and social enterprises is quite extensive. Much has been written about a definition of social entrepreneurs and social enterprises (Boschee and McClurg 2003; Dees 1998b). Case studies of social enterprises are beginning to become more prevalent (Alvord *et al.* 2004; Boschee 2001; Emerson and Twersky 1996; Massarsky and Beinhacker 2002; Shaw *et al.* 2002), and many are available through websites on social entrepreneurs.[1] Taken as a whole, the research on social enterprise and social entrepreneurs demonstrates the ability of nonprofits to undertake commercial endeavors. However, little is written about environmental organizations attempting similar practices. The research does not address organizations and entrepreneurs undertaking social and environmental value creation as traditional businesses or crossing definitional boundaries.

Research into alliances between nonprofit organizations and businesses attempts to fill in the aforementioned void. Some alliances demonstrate strong linkages between traditional businesses and environmental and social issues. Most of the research, however, does not focus on the benefits of such linkages. Some attempt to show how business and nonprofit alliances benefit environmental causes through **green alliances** (Arts 2002; Austin 2000; Austin *et al.* 2007; Dacin *et al.* 2007). However, the majority of the research reviews only cases of alliances, forgoing any analysis of costs or benefits (Bendell 2000; Yates 2007). Overall, the existing research into nonprofit and for-profit alliances appears to be beneficial in understanding only some of the aspects of hybrid organizations.

The case studies and definitions of social entrepreneurship and social enterprises can be quite useful as a guide to understanding hybrids, but the focus on nonprofits limits the scope of the research. As noted earlier, the majority of the research focuses on social issues, for the most

---

1 See, for example, Ashoka (www.ashoka.org/fellows, accessed May 7, 2009) and Schwab Foundation for Social Entrepreneurship (www.schwabfound.org/sf/SocialEntrepreneurs/index.htm, accessed May 7, 2009).

part ignoring environmental issues. Hybrid organizations often encompass both social and environmental concerns, and the current research is minimal in this area.

Literature summary

The research on hybrid organizations is relatively new. The concept of organizations crossing the boundaries between for-profits and nonprofits has appeared in the literature only recently. Some have posited that this requires a new legal definition beyond the stringent nonprofit/for-profit delineations (Billitteri 2007; Etchart and Davis 2003; Posner and Malani 2006). Others have expressed interest in creating a new business model to encompass this emerging field (Birkin *et al.* 2007, 2009; Engen 2005).[2] A few case studies have been written about hybrid organizations, emphasizing the viability of this new form, but do not offer deep analysis of the organizations (Cooney 2006; Hudnut *et al.* 2006). A few authors have attempted to show the importance of organizations that bridge nonprofits and for-profits, but they have not given a comprehensive picture of what constitutes a hybrid (Brandsen *et al.* 2005; Davis 1998; Hockerts 2003; Johnson 2000; Strom 2007).

Overall, new research is needed into hybrid organizations. The following analysis of practitioners and their activities in this field will go a long way towards understanding the formation of hybrids, their environmental practices, and how they are adding value while attempting to solve some of the most pressing issues facing the world today.

---

2   See also Corporation 2020, "New Principles of Corporate Design"; www.corporation2020. org, accessed January 30, 2009.

3
Uncovering the layers

To gain insights into for-profit, mission-driven companies, we utilized two primary data-gathering methods. The first was a survey of hybrid companies to capture broad-based trends within this sector of hybrid organizations. The second was a series of in-depth case studies of best-in-class companies, selected from the pool of respondents, to illustrate the unique characteristics of successful hybrid organizations. The methods for conducting the survey and case studies are described below.

Project definitions and hybrid organization criteria

To determine the criteria for selecting the hybrid organizations included in this study, the research team agreed on working definitions of hybrid organizations and environmental sustainability as follows.

Hybrid organization

A market-oriented and common-good mission-centered organization. Hybrid organizations may exhibit the following characteristics:

- Non-financial performance valuation

- Privately held by connected, individual investors

- Sub-market rates of return

- Alternative capitalization

Further discussion and illustration of the elements that characterize hybrid organizations are given below:

- **Market-oriented**: hybrid organizations are legally registered as business entities, as opposed to nonprofit entities. More importantly, products or services are provided in the marketplace at competitive prices rather than below cost as nonprofits often do

- **Common-good mission-centered**: hybrid organizations' actions and decision-making are explicitly linked to the mission. Further, this mission relates to contributing to an explicit common good (e.g., combating climate change)

- **Non-financial performance valuation**: as part of the blending of value in a hybrid organization, non-financial performance may be valued explicitly

- **Privately held by a connected set of shareholders**: hybrid organizations may be beholden to investors that buy into their mission and purpose rather than to common financial markets.[1] Many of the hybrid companies are controlled by individuals, families, or personally connected individuals

- **Sub-market rates of return**: while they must be profitable to be sustainable, hybrid organizations may continually or perpetually under-perform in the financial arena, relative to market rates

- **Alternative capitalization**: hybrid organizations may tap into non-traditional, below-market-rate financing mechanisms

---

1 We made the conscious decision to limit sample companies to privately held companies, ignoring publicly traded companies. Clearly this introduces a sampling bias; however, the rationale for this decision (as noted in Table 3) is that publicly traded companies have a legal fiduciary responsibility that prevents an organization from pursuing a common-good mission at the possible expense of financial performance.

Environmental sustainability

Environmental sustainability is commonly defined as: meeting today's natural resource needs while allowing future generations to meet their own needs (WCED 1987). Using the definition developed by the University of Michigan's Center for Sustainable Systems,[2] we narrowed the definition of environmental sustainability mission-driven companies to encompass only those whose direct business activities (products or services) or most significant inputs, raw materials, or resources contribute to one or more of the following:

- Clean air
- Clean energy
- Clean water
- Sustainable food or agricultural systems
- Sustainable housing

Due to time constraints and availability of data, we further restricted the companies selected to participate in the research according to the criteria specified in Table 3.

TABLE 3 Hybrid company selection criteria

Criteria	Rationale
For–profit companies only	Aligns with research gap identified in literature review
No restriction on size, revenue, or age	Desire to gain comprehensive insights on sector
No intermediaries, consulting companies, or investing companies	Desire to focus on practitioners in the hybrid sector to optimize lessons learned from those "on the ground"
No organizations with publicly traded shares (subsidiary of public company permitted)	Desire to focus on private companies, without legal fiduciary responsibility to shareholders

2 "Our Definition and Approach"; css.snre.umich.edu/makeframe.php?content=1_8_ approach, accessed March 23, 2008.

Survey analysis

Based on the *McKinsey 7-S Framework* (Rasiel and Friga 2001) and Andrew Hoffman's "The Object of Change" (Hoffman 2006), we selected the following five-category framework for the survey so as to develop a broad understanding of the hybrid organization:

- Business model and strategy
- Finance
- Organization, including structure, leadership, culture, and mission
- Processes and metrics
- Innovation

Using the above criteria, we identified 160 potential hybrid organizations via personal contacts, consultation with researchers, and manual internet searching, and approached them to participate in the survey. Although 87 companies agreed to participate, the total number of actual respondents completing the questionnaire was 47 (see the Appendix for a list of all companies included in the analysis). This represents a 54% rate of successful completion, and, more importantly, a large enough sample for statistical analysis.[3]

On the whole, the survey respondents varied widely. They included everything from small entrepreneurial start-ups such as ClearFuels Technology and Affirm-Aware to large, well-established companies such as Burt's Bees and Stonyfield Farm. However, the 47 respondents tended to skew towards small, young companies. The median number of employees in these companies was 20, and the companies' median age was only seven years old. In addition, annual revenues ranged from $0 to more than $2.3 billion, while the median annual revenue was approximately $1.5 million.

The companies themselves were mostly U.S.-based, with a handful of responses from other countries, including Canada, Brazil, and India. More than half of the respondents self-identified themselves as being devoted to clean energy, while only 10% were dedicated to addressing sustainable housing. From a financial perspective, while almost half of all respondents cited confidentiality for not disclosing their profitability, the data

---

3 Common data analysis requires a statistical $n \geq 30$.

set included some unprofitable companies as well as very profitable ones (> 20% profitability).

Table 4 highlights some of the key demographics of our sample set of hybrid respondents.

TABLE 4 Key demographics of the survey respondents

Characteristics	Range	Mean	Median
Company age:	1–40 years	10 years	7 years
Annual revenue:	$0 to $2.3 billion	$31.7 million	$1.5 million
No. of employees:	1–5,130	61	20
Other characteristics			
Headquarters:	North America, South America, Europe, Asia 80% U.S.–based		
Profitability:	<0% to >20% 50% cite confidentiality		
Environmental focus:	• 50% clean energy • 40% clean air • 40% sustainable food/agriculture • 35% clean water • 10% sustainable housing		

To study the responses submitted by the 47 companies, we conducted analysis using three primary techniques:

- **Polling and scaling analysis:** compilation and breakdown of responses for each question, accompanied by simple statistics and descriptions of the significant aspects as well as preliminary hypotheses of trend

- **Regression analysis:** perform regressions searching for significant correlations between variables rationally identified to be potential relationships of interest. For example, we ran a regression on aggregated responses to questions about funding sources and profitability

- **Qualitative analysis:** examination of each open-ended response for observable patterns and trends, noteworthy information, or need to follow up

Company study selection and outreach

We used two key criteria to determine the best-in-class companies from among all survey participants:

1. Environmental stewardship

2. Profitability

The responses from four specific survey questions were used to short-list the best-in-class candidates:

- Was the firm founded with environmental stewardship in mind?
  - 86% were founded with environmental mission

- Does the firm integrate environmental progress throughout the organization?
  - 83% were fully integrated

- Does the firm track environmental metrics?
  - 55% track internal *and* either up/downstream environmental performance

- What is your margin of profitability?
  - 50% have achieved some level of profitability[4]

Nine out of the 47 companies met all four environmental stewardship and profitability screens. These were:

- Burt's Bees

- Eden Foods

- Guayakí

- JASCO Organics

- Maggie's Organics

- Method

- PAX Scientific

- SUN OVENS International

- Zam-Bee-A Honey, Inc.

---

4 This percentage is among those respondents willing to disclose their margin of profitability.

Of these nine, we selected the following five organizations for further investigation:

- Eden Foods
- Guayakí
- Maggie's Organics
- PAX Scientific
- SUN OVENS

Although any of the nine companies would have made for insightful case studies, the selection of these five was influenced by breadth of their environmental mission, profitability, company ownership, and quality of survey responses.

Interviews

To develop the case studies, we had extensive communication with senior management and founders through visits to company headquarters and follow-up phone interviews. Interviewers raised a consistent set of questions and topics to assure consistency and comparability across case studies. Additionally, interviewers probed unique aspects of each business to allow company representatives to discuss firm-specific innovations. Information from secondary literature augmented the data gathered during the interviews.

Hybrid trends and lessons

This chapter describes the key themes and organizational trends from the survey. The following criteria helped identify the most notable trends and themes:

- Importance of trend to hybrid organizations
- Variances from expected results

Nine hybrid organization trends

The survey responses showed a variety of responses, some expected and some surprises. Nine key trends were identified as shown in Table 5.

Trend 1. Hybrids believe they do something completely different from competitors

From a game theory perspective, it is expected that hybrid organizations may have to define completely new strategies and redefine markets in order to be successful. As shown in Table 6, the survey results indeed illustrate this: most of the companies identified their business strategy as either 1) playing a new game in a new market, or 2) playing a new game in an established market. In fact, 66% of respondents claimed they were trying to do something completely different than their competitors.

TABLE 5 Summary of hybrid trends

Organizational characteristic	Observed pattern for hybrid organizations	% of respondents
Business model and strategy	1. Hybrids believe they do something completely different from competitors	66%
	2. Innovative product and environmental features are sources of competitive advantage	49%, 45% respectively
Finance	1. Hybrids have both positive and negative profit margins	50/50 split[a]
	2. Significant portions of hybrid funding comes from patient capital	59%
	3. Financing for hybrids can be both an advantage and disadvantage	33%, 25% respectively
Organization	1. Hybrids are led by transformational or participative leaders	75%
	2. Hybrids believe they have "fully integrated environmental sustainability"	83%
Processes and metrics	1. Some hybrids track environmental metrics	55%
Innovation	1. Hybrids have "notable innovations" relating to product or service	65%

[a] Almost half of all respondents were unwilling to disclose their margin of profitability.

TABLE 6 Respondent strategies

		Strategic gameboard			
		Where they compete			
		Established market	New market	Other	Total
How they compete	Same game	13%	4%	11%	28%
	New game	26%	30%	11%	66%
	Other	2%	0%	4%	6%
	Total	40%	34%	26%	100%

As supported by the case studies, however, it should be noted that while a hybrid organization may start out carving new territory, often it is not long before fast-followers move in.

> SpringStar provides effective, non-toxic and environmentally safe pest control products; it's a new way to do an old thing — organic food is analogous. **William Pickard, CFO, SpringStar**

Trend 2. Innovative product, environmental features are sources of competitive advantage

Recent literature suggests that there is a growing market for "green" products. Therefore, we expected that hybrid organizations might cater to this customer segment, and would use some combination of environmental features or branding as a source of competitive advantage versus industry peers.

TABLE 7 Mean rank of sources of competitive advantage

From 1 to 6, 1 = highest

Innovative product/ service	Higher quality	Environmental features	Brand name	Lower cost
2.7	2.9	3.0	3.8	3.9

TABLE 8 Top and bottom most common sources of competitive advantage

Source of competitive advantage	Ranked in top two	Ranked in bottom two
Brand name	21%	38%
Environmental features	45%	17%
Higher quality	40%	15%
Innovative product	49%	11%
Low cost	30%	47%
Other	9%	13%

Table 7 shows the sources of competitive advantage for the respondents as a whole. On average, innovative product/service and higher-quality products were the two most important overall advantages for hybrid organizations. However, the two sources that companies most often ranked first or second were innovative product and environmental features (see Table 8). The two sources most often ranked last and second last were brand name and low cost.

Table 8 reveals two trends: (1) low cost differentiation is not a strategy used by successful hybrids, and, conversely (2) developing premium products or premium segments can be a successful strategy.

> Our all-natural composition [an environmental feature] is a significant competitive advantage. **Yola Carlough, Director of Sustainability, Burt's Bees**

Trend 3. Hybrids have both positive and negative profit margins

FIGURE 4 Profitability margin

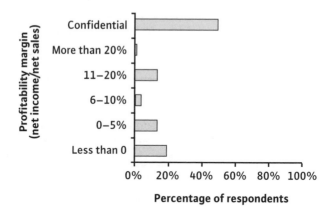

Prior to reviewing the survey results, the team believed that hybrid organizations might have limits to profitability in order to meet their environmental mission. But the survey data show that 50% of the hybrid companies willing to disclose their profitability were actually profitable (see Fig. 4). Of these, their aggregated return was below market rate (i.e., below the Dow Jones long-term average return of 11%).

While these results suggest that financial viability is difficult to achieve in a hybrid organization, it is crucial to recall that traditional for-profit businesses also have high rates of failure, especially during start-up or early-stage development — the survey respondent companies were relatively young, with an average age of seven years. Indeed, the respondent answers show that the older the hybrid organization, the greater the likelihood to be profitable.

Trend 4. Significant portions of financing for hybrids come from patient capital

TABLE 9 Sources of financing

Type of financing	Level of financing						Weighted average
	0%	1–20%	21–40%	41–60%	61–80%	81–100%	
Traditional market–rate equity	26%	4%	0%	6%	9%	11%	24%
Traditional market–rate debt	17%	13%	6%	4%	6%	2%	15%
Below market–rate debt	26%	0%	4%	2%	0%	0%	3%
Below market–rate equity	23%	4%	0%	4%	4%	2%	9%
Grants	19%	19%	13%	0%	0%	2%	10%
Founder(s), friends, or family	15%	23%	9%	2%	6%	11%	25%
Reinvestment of operating profits	19%	17%	4%	4%	2%	4%	13%

The survey results show that, overall, 59% of the respondents' financing comes from patient capital sources, while 12% comes from "below market-rate" equity or debt[1] (see Table 9).

1 Patient capital includes: below-market-rate debt and equity; grants; founder(s), friends, or family; and reinvestment of operating profits.

We had expected that a significant proportion of hybrid organizations would be financed from patient funds, but the magnitude of the result is nonetheless notably high. The 12% presence of below-market-rate funds seems to demonstrate the emergence of an alternative funding source, one that perhaps more and more mission-driven organizations will be able to tap into in the future. Moreover, the 59% figure suggests that investors buying into these hybrid organizations may have returns on investment expectations that are balanced with or include environmental performance returns.

> Patient financing is an advantage that "allows us time and flexibility to test and de-risk our model rather than having to rush to market to earn profits." **Sagun Saxena, CEO, CleanStar Energy**

Trend 5. Financing hybrids can be both an advantage and disadvantage

FIGURE 5 Financing as a source of advantage or challenge in meeting environmental goals

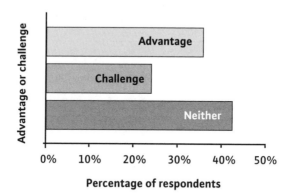

Although we hypothesized that hybrids may have an advantage over traditional firms by appealing to alternative sources of capital such as patient investors, the survey results show that sources of financing can be both a significant advantage and disadvantage to hybrid organizations; almost one-third of respondents see their sources of financing as an advantage in achieving their environmental sustainability goals (see Fig. 5). Some quotes from these responses are as follows:

> Advantage in that we are playing the "long game" because, as water use increases, so does scarcity and business opportunities. **Stephen Hinton, Managing Director, Purity**

> Since we do not have public or outside equity stakeholders, we do not have quarterly profit pressures. **Jenn Orgolini, Sustainability Director, New Belgium Brewing Company**

> Yes, many of our investors are focused on clean tech and are looking for both financial and social/environmental returns on their investment. **Ned Tozun, President, D.light Design**

For those hybrids where financing is a source of challenge, the following responses exemplify the types of associated drawbacks.

> Investing in environmentally friendly equipment and supplies, and sustainably grown fair trade ingredients for our products, while trying to competitively price our products, took away from the amount of marketing and advertising campaigns we would have liked to roll out at times. We had to compromise and find alternatives. **Constance Duke, President, JASCO Organics**

> We have had some success approving capital projects by accounting for payback, reduced operating costs, positive brand implications, etc. But competition for capital dollars is tight, and in a company for which meeting growth targets is critical to the next year's funding allocation, projects that will increase manufacturing capacity or productivity sometimes prevail over projects with environmental rationale but longer paybacks. **Nancy Hirshberg, Vice President of Natural Resources, Stonyfield Farm**

Trend 6. Hybrids are led by transformational or participative leaders

FIGURE 6 Leadership style of CEOs

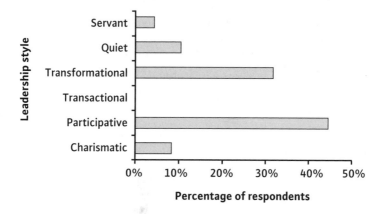

We expected that many hybrid organizations would be led by charismatic, inspiring leaders, especially because hybrids place significant emphasis on mission.[2] However, Figure 6 shows that 75% of leaders were identified as "participative" or "transformational." None of the leaders of hybrid organizations in the survey was described as "transactional." This suggests hybrids tend to be led by executives who have a collaborative management style rather than the command-and-control style prevalent in older and more traditional firms.

> Michael's [CEO] door is always open. He doesn't always agree, but is willing to take time to look at your idea. **Sue Becker, Vice President of Marketing and Sales, Eden Foods**

2 Leadership styles offered in the questionnaire were as follows: Charismatic: gathers followers through personality and charm, rather than formal power or authority; Participative: extroverted, sensitive leader who openly shares decisions and authority with subordinates; Transactional: leads by reward and punishment, with a clear chain of command; Transformational: inspiring leader through vision and passion, achieving success by clarity of thought and articulation; Quiet: success based not on ego and character but thoughts and actions; Servant: leads by serving others, rather than others serving the leader, emphasizing collaboration and trust.

Trend 7. Hybrids believe they have "fully integrated environmental sustainability"

FIGURE 7 Integration of environmental sustainability

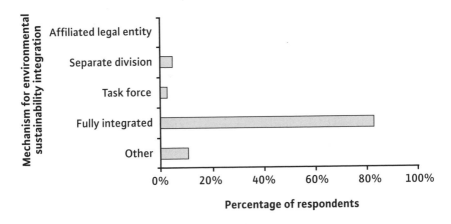

Percentage of respondents

The survey responses also show that 83% of respondents believe environmental sustainability is "fully integrated" throughout their organizations (see Fig. 7). In contrast to organizations that set up a separate division or a task force, hybrid organizations tend to integrate environmental sustainability across all departments and functions. This approach speaks to the strong emphasis on environmental sustainability in the business model and strategy.

> The mission-first nature of our organizational structure has been a source of advantage in achieving environmental sustainability goals because the founders have set lofty personal environmental goals that radiate down through the company.
> **Dylan Rapp, General Manager, Reforest Teak**

Trend 8. Some hybrids track environmental metrics

FIGURE 8 Environmental metrics tracking

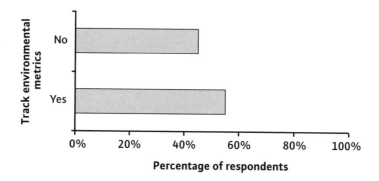

We expected that hybrid organizations would often track the environmental performance of suppliers, customers, and internal operations. But while most respondents stated they fully integrated environmental sustainability throughout their organization, only 55% actually tracked environmental metrics (see Fig. 8). For those that do track sustainability, 85% use in-house tools, as opposed to some other standard or certification.

These results are surprising for two reasons. First, 55% is lower than expected given the recent wave of CSR reports, agreements, and initiatives that have flooded the market. One possible rationale for this relatively low percentage is that CSR reports are used in large part by publicly held companies to communicate to shareholders. Privately held hybrids have little need for such explicit external communication because owners, employees, and customers have already bought into their mission. In addition, the fact that more than half of all respondents indicated that they track the metrics of either their supplier or their customers indicates that the majority of hybrid organizations tend to have strong relationships across their supply chain. This indication is backed by evidence from several of the case studies.

Second, while 83% of respondents believe environmental sustainability is fully integrated, only 55% actually track environmental metrics. This begs the question: If one is not tracking metrics, how does one know that they are making progress? One potential answer is that, in some hybrids, environmental sustainability is so grounded throughout the organization that there is no need for metrics. Another possible explanation is that many hybrids simply lack the resources to perform this measurement and that the very nature of the business ensures environmental steward-ship as a whole. The responses show evidence of belief in both these possible explanations.

Trend 9. Hybrids have "notable innovations" relating to product or service

FIGURE 9 Notable innovations

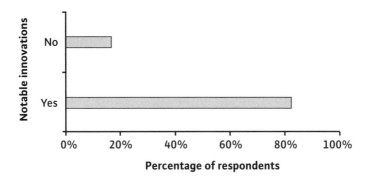

A "notable innovation" was claimed by 83% of respondents (see Fig. 9); approximately 80% of these innovations were product- or technology-related.

Some examples of product innovations from respondents include the following:

> Patented approach using floating (lighter-than-air) rotors that rise to 1,000 ft on a tether. Wind spins the rotor on a horizontal axis and electricity is generated. Electrical energy is transferred down the tether for storage or use. **Tony Asterita, Co-founder, Magenn Power**

> (1) Mud frame beehives built with locally available resources . . . [and] . . . (2) ability to lighten/process beeswax using locally available materials, with no additives, even organic-approved additives. **Jenny Gelber, CFO & Owner, Zam-Bee-A Honey, Inc.**

Some examples of business model innovations include:

> Our personal relationships with all of our growers and their families. **Michael Potter, President, Eden Foods**

> Enabling poor women in the developing world to obtain Sun Ovens and pay for them in small weekly installments using a portion of the money saved by not buying charcoal or other cooking fuels. **Paul M. Munsen, President, SUN OVENS International**

> Raw material pricing/sourcing based on a RESTORATION model that is leading to reforestation of the land from which we are sourcing yerba mate. **Pierre Ferrari, Director, VP Marketing and Sales, Guayakí**

It is clear from the survey results that hybrid organizations exhibit a substantial amount of variance when it comes to organizational function and execution. However, it is also clear that they believe themselves to be treading new ground in the products and services they offer, as compared with traditional for-profit competitors.

Further, the finding that almost 60% of the survey respondents have some sort of patient capital funding supports the notion that hybrid organizations, as well as their financers, believe in blending non-financial performance and financial performance. The variance found in profitability also supports the notion that hybrids may under-perform relative to market rates, although again it should be reiterated that the respondents' age was skewed towards younger enterprises, so current profitability margins may not necessarily bear any resemblance to their long-term profitability.

5

CASE STUDY
SUN OVENS International — patient dealmaker

Introduction

SUN OVENS International, Inc., based in Elburn, IL, provides cooking energy solutions to the world's poor. However, it struggles to meet its environmental and profitability goals. With but six employees making and distributing solar ovens around the world and a myriad of business risks all across its value chain, it is clear that the key to the success of SUN OVENS is patience in all aspects of its business in order to meet both sets of corporate goals. See Table 10 for an overview of the company.

While being loyal to the non-financial mission of an organization is common in all hybrid organizations, the extent to which SUN OVENS has done so — particularly in light of significant financial pressures — is distinctly uncommon. The company has pursued a small and challenging market (solar ovens), chased fleeting sources of revenue (Y2K emergency preparedness), and ventured close to bankruptcy (employees providing personal capital into the company). From staying the course in volatile political markets, to finding the right entrepreneur in developing countries, to fending off offers to buy the company's assets, SUN OVENS has managed to stay true to its environmental objectives while turning around its operational efficiency.

TABLE 10 SUN OVENS overview

SUN OVENS International in 2008	
Year founded:	1998
Annual revenue:	$700,000
No. of employees:	6
Headquarters:	Elburn, IL, USA
Environmental focus:	• Clean air • Clean energy
Profitability level:	Positive operating margin

Mission statement

SUN OVENS International, Inc. is striving to develop and implement comprehensive solar cooking programs that will radically decrease the developing world's dependence on fuel wood and dung as the primary cooking fuels while benefiting the environment, raising the standard of living, and improving the health of the poor worldwide.

After a deeper analysis, it becomes clear that this unwavering commitment and steadfastness in the face of ongoing business challenges comes from two sources: patience and morality, or, more specifically, the patience and morality of Paul Munsen, President of SUN OVENS International.

Overview and history

Industry overview: cooking in developing countries

In developing countries, particularly in rural areas, approximately 2.5 billion people rely on biomass sources, including firewood, charcoal, animal dung, and agricultural waste to meet their needs for cooking energy. In many countries, these resources account for more than 90% of household energy consumption (IEA 2006).

While biomass is not a cause for concern in and of itself, it does have significant adverse consequences for individual health, the environment, and economic development when it is unsustainably harvested and when energy conversion techniques are inefficient. Approximately 1.3 million people — the majority of whom are women and children — die prematurely each year due to exposure from biomass indoor air pollution. Fuel collection takes away time and effort that could be spent on education or other income-generating activities. The ongoing cost of fuel can represent up to half of all household expenditures. Moreover, environmental harms such as land degradation and regional air pollution often result from unplanned harvesting.

One set of solutions to address these problems lies in solar-powered ovens. Cooking with charcoal in a covered environment can have the same harmful effect on the human respiratory tract as smoking three packs of cigarettes per day; solar ovens can actually create lasting financial and beneficial health effects.

Background information

SUN OVENS® was developed in 1986 by Tom Burns, a retired restaurateur from Milwaukee, WI, who was very active with Rotary International, a group that remains involved with the company today. From his experience in operating restaurants, he knew a great deal about cooking and, from his international travel, he became aware of the growing problem of deforestation. Tom took a concept that had been around for centuries and engineered into it more recently developed materials to produce an effective solar cooking device.

From 1986 to 1997, SUN OVENS® were made and marketed by Burns Milwaukee, Inc. Since that time, thousands of portable models have been shipped to more than 125 countries around the globe. SUN OVENS® have helped feed refugees in relocation camps, aboriginals in remote villages, workers at field sites, climbers on the slopes of Mount Everest, and soldiers during the Persian Gulf War.

In 1998, Paul Munsen took over company leadership, formed SUN OVENS International, Inc. and moved manufacturing from Milwaukee to Elburn, IL (40 miles west of Chicago). SUN OVENS International, Inc. has expanded the use of its ovens by making them more widely available in the U.S. and around the world. Assembly plants to make GLOBAL SUN OVENS® have been established in a number of developing countries to reduce the cost of production and the cost of shipping to the people that need them the most.

Goals and objectives

SUN OVENS strives to develop and implement comprehensive solar cooking programs that will radically decrease the developing world's dependence on biomass as the primary cooking fuels, ultimately benefiting the environment, raising the standard of living, and improving the health of the poor worldwide. Moreover, up to two-thirds of the world's population wake up every morning not knowing if they will eat at night;[1] with more than two billion people living on less than two dollars per day, there is ample opportunity to provide energy for cooking while reducing household expenses all over the world.

Product information

SUN OVENS manufactures two types of solar ovens:

1. VILLAGER SUN OVEN®

2. GLOBAL SUN OVEN®

Both of these, as well as the term SUN OVEN®, are registered trademarks of the company. The VILLAGER SUN OVEN® is designed for large-scale feeding situations that require cooking great volumes of food quickly, capable of making up to 1,200 meals per day or 28 loaves of bread per hour. Even though it is called an oven, enormous quantities of food can be boiled, steamed, or baked at cooking temperatures of up to 500°F/260°C with no fuel costs. Alternatively, it can be run on a 20 lb propane tank for 12 straight hours.

The GLOBAL SUN OVEN® has been devised to meet up to 70% of the needs of a family of six to eight people in a developing country. This portable box (approximately eight cubic feet) keeps in moisture and air, thereby ensuring hot meals well after sundown. It is guaranteed for 15 years of everyday use. Figure 10 shows a photograph of a GLOBAL SUN OVEN® and Figure 11 is a schematic diagram illustrating its components.

---

1 Personal communication with P. Munsen, Elburn, IL, January 18, 2008.

FIGURE 10 Photograph of a GLOBAL SUN OVEN®

FIGURE 11 Schematic drawing of a GLOBAL SUN OVEN® and its component
        parts

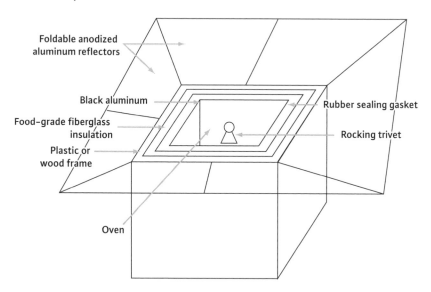

SUN OVENS' technology is very simple, and the design has not changed since its original design in the 1980s. The ovens consist of collapsible aluminum panel reflectors that redirect sunlight into a well-insulated box (the oven). The box itself consists of a plastic shell, one-inch-thick food-grade fiberglass insulation, and an interior black aluminum container that serves as the oven walls. A rocking trivet inside the oven allows food to remain level if the oven is jostled. A glass plate on top of the box locks the heated air inside the oven, and a proprietary gasket ensures the food never dries out and remains hot for many hours after sundown.

Business strategy and model

SUN OVENS currently serves two primary markets:

- Developed-country markets

- Developing-country markets

Prior to incorporation, SUN OVENS mainly sold its products via partnerships with international non-governmental organizations (NGOs) such as Rotary International to overseas markets. After incorporation, SUN OVENS shifted its geographic markets and changed its core business model, as described in more detail below. Figure 12 shows how SUN OVENS' strategy has shifted since incorporation.

FIGURE 12 SUN OVENS' strategic positioning

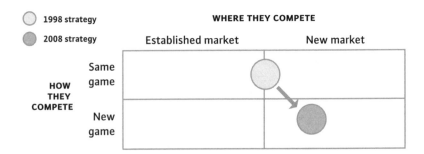

SUN OVENS market

Developed–country markets

SUN OVENS sells both models in developed countries, but primarily GLOBAL SUN OVENS® to the following consumer groups in the U.S., Canada, Australia, Japan, Spain, and Germany:

- **Green consumers**: these eco-conscious consumers want to purchase energy-efficient appliances, and/or often recreate outdoors
- **Food enthusiasts**: these "foodies" claim solar ovens offer more flavor and juicier, all-natural tastes
- **Emergency preparedness**: these are individual, commercial, or retail customers who recognize the need for a cooking mechanism when electricity is no longer available (e.g., hurricanes, floods, etc.)

Despite its core business in ovens, SUN OVENS has plans to expand the portfolio of offerings available on its website by partnering with other solar-inspired manufacturers to increase domestic revenue generation. New products to be sold include a solar-inspired cookbook (retailing for approximately $12) and solar-powered headlamp (retailing for approximately $30). A third product that may be offered in the future is a solar-powered water pasteurizer.

Developing–country markets

In developing countries, SUN OVENS either licenses its GLOBAL SUN OVENS® to local entrepreneurs who ultimately sell to poor families willing to replace their wood-/dung-based cooking equipment, or it sells to large international NGOs who distribute these ovens to people in need.

Although the investment in solar cookers can be significant for end-customers (the two billion people living on less than two dollars per day), the combination of product effectiveness, improved air quality, time savings, and avoided fuel costs often convinces consumers that SUN OVENS' products are worth the investment. Most consumers are women because they are most often the ones actually doing the cooking.

Historically, SUN OVENS' primary focus has been the Middle East (Jordan), Africa (Nigeria, Kenya, Uganda), and the Caribbean (Dominican

Republic, Haiti). In rare instances, SUN OVENS sells its ovens to middle-class consumers in developing economies as a backup power source for electricity-based ovens. The company also sells its VILLAGER SUN OVENS® to orphanages, schools, and hospitals in developing countries.

Business model

SUN OVENS has created a GLOBAL SUN OVEN® assembly system that enables assembly on location. Local assembly dramatically reduces the oven price and can also create local jobs, all the while getting ovens into the hands of the people who need them most. Local assembly often reduces the price approximately 50% compared to U.S. retail prices, and, when locally sourced materials are employed, the price can be reduced another 10–30%.[2]

SUN OVENS designs and builds its products in Elburn, IL, and typically manufactures these ovens in batch cycles. As illustrated in Figure 11, the ovens themselves are simply designed, minimizing the number and complexity of components where possible. Such design enables easy transfer of engineering knowledge to developing-country markets as described below.

Not only is the product itself designed with the poor in mind, but production as well:

- The fixtures it uses are made of wood
- The hand tools used can all be replaced by simple low-tech tools in developing countries (screwdrivers and rivet guns)
- Equipment can be operated without electricity if necessary (i.e., hand-powered).

"Everything is designed to be transferable," says Paul Munsen.[3] While the production is not ISO-certified, SUN OVENS does have a production manual written to ISO standards (e.g., each production step has a planned and monitored task duration).

Figure 13 illustrates the different business models for both of SUN OVENS' customer markets. These are described in more detail below.

---

2 SUN OVENS' estimates.
3 Personal communication with P. Munsen, Elburn, IL, January 18, 2008.

FIGURE 13 Comparison of SUN OVENS business models for developed and developing-country markets

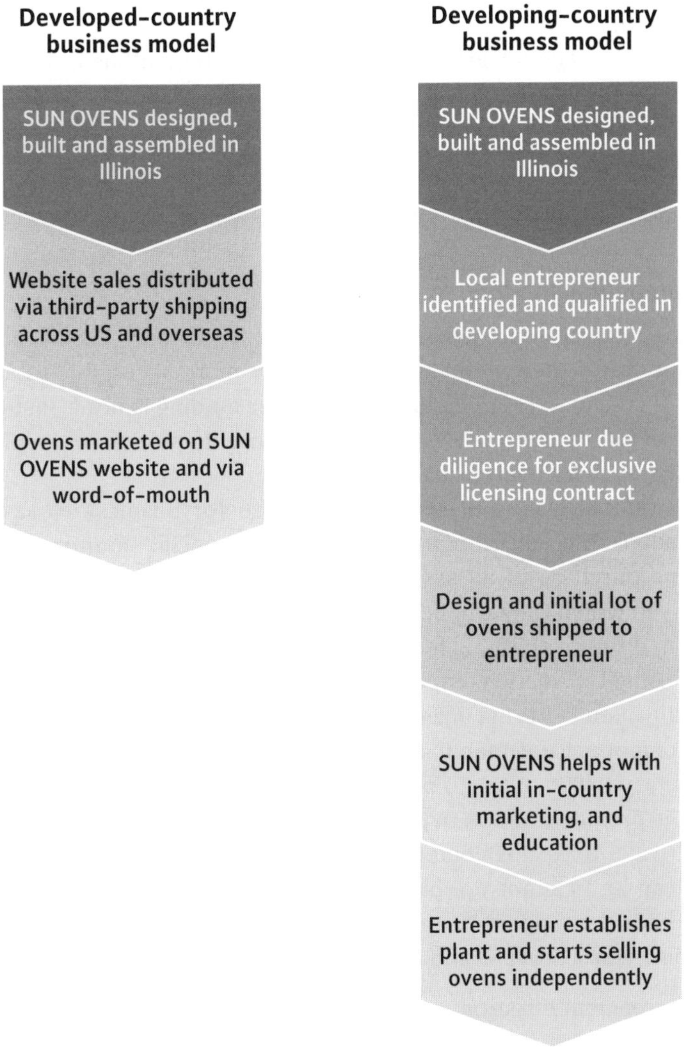

Developed-country business model

Developing-country business model

Developed-country business model	Developing-country business model
SUN OVENS designed, built and assembled in Illinois	SUN OVENS designed, built and assembled in Illinois
Website sales distributed via third-party shipping across US and overseas	Local entrepreneur identified and qualified in developing country
Ovens marketed on SUN OVENS website and via word-of-mouth	Entrepreneur due diligence for exclusive licensing contract
	Design and initial lot of ovens shipped to entrepreneur
	SUN OVENS helps with initial in-country marketing, and education
	Entrepreneur establishes plant and starts selling ovens independently

In developed countries, SUN OVENS sells the GLOBAL SUN OVEN® as niche products in energy-conscious markets. SUN OVENS has had several conversations to supply large retailers in the U.S. but the price points are wrong. SUN OVENS' wholesale price is too high for these retailers, who demand substantial profit margins from their suppliers. Instead, SUN OVENS sells through retailers who want drop shipping and are therefore willing to accept a lower profit margin. As a whole, SUN OVENS does its current sales via its website, online dealers (those that order five or more ovens), and niche retailers.

In developing countries, SUN OVENS has two different business models:

- Entrepreneurial model
- NGO model

These are detailed in turn below.

Entrepreneurial model

The aim of the entrepreneurial model is to drive as much cost as possible from the price, thereby making the product more accessible to a wider group of consumers. Recognizing that donor funding is not a sustainable source of funding, SUN OVENS prefers to license its product to local entrepreneurs in an innovative arrangement.

SUN OVENS starts by licensing a private-sector business to assemble U.S.-made ovens and to market them in one specific country. With the one-time purchase of an assembly package, ovens can be made in the country in which they will be used, dramatically reducing the cost of the ovens and future shipping fees. Once an assembly plant has been established using U.S.-made components, specifications are provided that will allow the manufacturing of any of the components to be done locally. The only component not manufactured locally is the gasket, which remains proprietary to SUN OVENS to prevent complete imitation of the ovens. The gasket is provided by SUN OVENS at a price that includes a small royalty.

SUN OVENS does not completely mandate what its licensed entrepreneurs can and cannot do, but does make suggestions on how to make their products "appeal to the masses" whenever possible.[4] Each contract between SUN OVENS and entrepreneur varies but typically covers:

- Agreement duration
- Chosen country or region
- Quantity of ovens to be sold
- Fees to be paid

4 Personal communication with P. Munsen, Elburn, IL, January 18, 2008.

The reality in many developing economies is that the market is simply not sufficiently aware or educated for its products, and the licensed entrepreneur sells to middle-class or military consumers.

A typical process for developing an entrepreneur in a new country might be as follows:

- SUN OVENS identifies a potential local entrepreneur in a country based on their business ability, in-country network of contacts, and appetite to make the business a success

- SUN OVENS provides specifications and costs to assemble and manufacture GLOBAL SUN OVENS®, including a confidential franchise fee

- If the entrepreneur can come up with the necessary cash and can show that they can sell a requisite number of ovens, an exclusive country-wide licensing contract is signed
  - This contract is country-wide because Paul Munsen recognized it would be impossible to enforce multiple geographic licenses within a single country
  - The contract stipulates a minimum number of ovens required to be sold per year, including a fixed number of assembled ovens (higher margin, lower per unit cost) from Illinois. This sales volume requirement prevents someone from obtaining the exclusive license and then not actually selling any ovens; such behavior would generate zero ongoing revenue from gasket sales or assembled oven sales
  - Contracts are *never* joint ventures because Paul has also recognized that North–South joint ventures usually result in the Southern partner depending more heavily on the Northern partner for financing and resources, ultimately resulting in a marriage of non-equals; Northern partners are perceived as "a tree that drips money"[5]
  - The minimum amount required on behalf of the entrepreneur is approximately $50,000, most of which is spent on building and shipping the initial batch of ovens overseas. The remainder is spent on setup, training, import tax, and raw materials of the local assembly plant (see the Finance section on pages 51ff. for further cost breakdown details)

5   Personal communication with P. Munsen, Elburn, IL, January 18, 2008.

- Once the first shipment has arrived, SUN OVENS staff may also arrive to help with marketing for initial product launch in-country (e.g., "U.S.A." branding) in order to command higher margins and generate initial cash flows

- A local community organization or NGO is sometimes involved to help train or educate local consumers. These organizations collaborate with the entrepreneur to make the entrepreneurial business model work

- Another possibility for partnership being explored in the entrepreneurial model is to involve the help of microfinance institutions. Such microfinancing could either help entrepreneurs avoid the incredibly high financing charges from major lending institutions (with interest rates sometimes upwards of 30%) or help consumers raise enough cash to finance the purchase of the oven[6]

NGO model

This model is based on the outreach and efforts of large international NGOs or private voluntary organizations (PVOs) because the challenges of implementing solar cooking projects are often more cultural than they are technical. The ovens themselves have been designed to overcome some of these cultural challenges, but the involvement of a local NGO or PVO that understands the needs and customs of the consumers (often women) using the ovens can often overcome lack of cooking knowledge of the entrepreneurs (often men).

SUN OVENS is looking to form working relationships with NGOs and PVOs in regions of the world blessed with an abundance of sunshine to develop and implement projects. In addition, the VILLAGER SUN OVEN® is

---

6 The Grameen Bank model would be ideal here since it is based on community banking and self-selection of credible community members. Moreover, the collective dependency of this setup also encourages weekly meetings to administer the finances, share learning, and obtain peer support. The International Finance Corporation has an environmental development program aimed at introducing new technologies in developing countries but programs such as these need to be based on microloans, not institutional loans.

often donated to schools and other organizations through the help of Rotary International.[7]

Historically, SUN OVENS focused on developing countries using the NGO model. However, this was recognized by Paul as unsustainable and the plan going forward is to focus on the entrepreneurial model in developing and transitional countries. Thus, only the VILLAGER SUN OVEN® continues to be sold via the NGO model. Accordingly, a large part of the marketing efforts for the VILLAGER SUN OVEN® is geared towards the donor, and not the consumer.

Competition

There are many different types and kinds of solar ovens. Some common types of solar ovens are listed in Table 11.

TABLE 11 Common types of solar oven

Category	Description
Cookits	Similar to solar ovens
HotPots	Dark pots inside clear outer pots
Parabolic solar ovens	Solar ovens that use parabolic reflectors which heat up food much quicker than traditional solar ovens
Solar kettles	Solar–thermal vacuum tubes used to heat liquids
Hybrid solar ovens	Combined solar box cookers and conventional heating elements
Hybrid solar grills	Adjustable parabolic reflector with grills and conventional fuel grills

Paul believes there are very few solar cookers that are actually viable alternatives to his company's products. Hybrid ovens, running on solar and conventional electricity, are an example of a competitive product achieving some levels of success in places such as India. Paul has cooked with both products side by side, and has found that the hybrids have

7   Tom Burns, the inventor of the SUN OVEN®, has been a member of Rotary International for more than 40 years. It was Tom's involvement in Rotary that showed him the need people around the world had for a way to cook that did not require cutting down trees. Rotary International remains an active participant in numerous projects around the world.

often required switchover to battery power while the SUN OVENS® worked perfectly well.

However, in addition to the technical differences, the main reason Paul believes hybrid ovens have a limited growth potential is because of their specific marketing needs: to showcase the benefits of hybrid ovens, one has to market the negatives of solar cooking. Not only does this require much more information to explain, but this ultimately defeats the purpose of selling solar ovens to begin with. SUN OVENS discontinued its hybrid model in 1998.

Another strong competitor product is the parabolic solar oven. These ovens heat up much faster than other solar ovens, but they also have several unique product risks. SUN OVENS does not make these products because of the risk of child blindness; because parabolic reflectors direct sunlight into one focal point, it is very easy for unsuspecting children or cooks to be blinded by the light. In addition, because of their high temperature, parabolic ovens must be constantly stirred to ensure the food does not burn; SUN OVENS' even convectional heating eliminates the need for stirring. However, these parabolic ovens have proved very successful in places like Mexico, where the need to fry tortillas is a good fit for these high-temperature ovens.

Paul believes SUN OVENS' products are more threatened by low-technology solar ovens, i.e., cardboard or other simplistic solar ovens. The nature of this threat is that low-tech ovens are not only less expensive, but are also often of poor quality and operation. People who have tried these low-quality ovens find they don't last longer than three months, and do not keep the food sufficiently warm. These "$15 solar ovens kill the market for $150 ovens," says Paul Munsen,[8] and this leads to a huge legacy problem once a product fails (see "Market risk" on pages 59ff.). The success of a SUN OVEN® is that "it takes in the best of everything into one unit."[9]

Paul believes that a focus on delivery and implementation will ultimately make SUN OVENS more profitable in the future. Indeed, price continues to be the key decision driver for many end-customers, and hence these lower-priced products of inferior quality continue to be the company's main source of competition.

To counter these lower price and quality legacies, SUN OVENS continues to put heavy emphasis on product education and on-the-ground demon-

---

8 Personal communication with P. Munsen, Elburn, IL, January 18, 2008.
9 *Ibid.*

strations — strategies that will hopefully pay off in the long term. On a product level basis, it is also clear that the proprietary gasket creates a distinct source of advantage over other solar ovens.

Finance

Sales and revenue

Developed-country sales have grown dramatically from 2006 to 2008. Partly due to increased global eco-awareness and partly due to a weakening U.S. dollar, sales to other developed countries such as Japan, Australia, Spain, and Germany have risen considerably. Overall, oven shipments rose 50% from 2006 to 2007, and in January 2008 shipments had doubled compared to January 2007.

Publicity from CNN, Business 2.0, and other media outlets created significant interest and buzz for the company in 2007 (for example, more than 150 people contacted Paul interested in investing in SUN OVENS after this series of media coverage) and the firm hopes to continue to capitalize on this publicity in the future. Its three-year plan aims to grow revenues from $0.75 million in 2007 to $10 million by 2010, and Paul is currently looking at the carbon trading markets for future sources of revenue to help both SUN OVENS and its licensed entrepreneurs.

As of early 2008, SUN OVENS has licensed assembly plants in Haiti, the Dominican Republic, and Ghana. In the past, SUN OVENS has delivered its products to Afghanistan, North Korea, Nepal, and South Africa. Plans are in the works to create licensed plants in Uganda, Morocco, and Nigeria, and SUN OVENS is in talks with 19 potential entrepreneurs. Paul expects that one-third of the entrepreneurs will actually sign a license contract with SUN OVENS. Plans for assembly plants in Kenya and Pakistan have had to be put on hold due to political instability.

Liabilities and obligations

Paul Munsen describes the SUN OVENS balance sheet as "more than bankrupt."[10] While SUN OVENS has never been fully profitable, it currently earns

---

10 Personal communication with P. Munsen, Elburn, IL, January 18, 2008.

a positive operating margin. Unfortunately, its balance sheet is weighed down by extensive debt obligations stemming from poor operations in its early years of incorporation. As shown in Figure 14, the upside of its financial situation is that these debtors do not expect market rates of return on their investments, and, accordingly, SUN OVENS can afford to be more patient in turning operating profit into net profit. Below are highlights that explain the poor balance sheet situation.

FIGURE 14 Breakdown of SUN OVENS' current funding

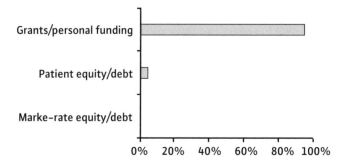

Poor beginnings

Tom Burns was a successful restaurateur in the Milwaukee area and started making SUN OVENS in 1986. He started the company with his own money, some outside investment, and a bank loan, eventually raising approximately $2.5 million to operate the company. Although Tom had a high potential product, email and internet were still unpopular modes of communication and distribution and, after 12 years of struggling to market his product, he decided to turn over the venture to someone else. At this time, Paul Munsen was brought in, particularly because of his marketing experience. With new investment when Paul came on in 1998, the bank was paid off. Subsequently, Paul incorporated the company, moved operations to Elburn, IL, and started doing promotions in Washington, DC as a way to tap into the international development market.

"My biggest mistake"

Looking at all the news around Y2K, Paul saw a huge opportunity to get into the Y2K[11] emergency preparedness business, and in 1999, the first full year after incorporating, SUN OVENS saw huge sales — of the order of $1.6 million, compared with $300,000 for the eight preceding months in 1998.

However, after 2000 went by without a hitch, many of the SUN OVENS dealers, who had expected huge revenues from Y2K failures, went bankrupt and left SUN OVENS with a large unpaid Accounts Receivable. This caused a cash flow problem leading to a large Accounts Payable and certain unpaid corporate taxes for SUN OVENS. In 2000, sales dropped precipitously to $185,000, and SUN OVENS was forced to liquidate inventory at or below cost, just to meet its cash flow and short-term obligations.

This began a pattern of managing the business based on cash flow, instead of profit. Cash flow was so tight that Paul was sometimes forced to forgo personal salary payments, to the point of refinancing his personal mortgage. Once only $3,000 away from being completely paid off, his home mortgage is now worth more than $100,000. SUN OVENS recently paid off the last remnant of debt from 1999 and it hopes to successfully pay off all owed vendors in the future.

Only cash on delivery

Due to poor credit standing, weak bargaining power, and insufficient cash flows, SUN OVENS is forced to pay for its parts with cash on delivery (COD); suppliers may be willing to supply the company but are unwilling to accept cash-flow risk themselves. This prepayment for materials restricts what the company can do since cash outlays have to be front-ended.

Further constricting the company's cash flow is the fact that it must pay a part price premium due to low-volume orders. This is particularly evident for one component, the plastic outer shell which, at low volumes, can cost as much as $15 per unit but at higher volumes can decrease to $7 per unit.

Cost structure

SUN OVENS' cost structure is based on a simple cost-plus-markup model. The markup depends on the end market being served, but Table 12 displays the current cost structure for the GLOBAL SUN OVEN®.

---

11 Also known as the Year 2000 problem or Millennium Bug.

TABLE 12 Comparison of cost structures for developed- and developing-country markets

All figures approximate USD

	Unit cost	
GLOBAL SUN OVEN® component	Domestic market	Overseas market
Total material cost out of Elburn (including shipping)	$95–110	$105–120
Local markup	$160[a]	$30–45[b]
Final retail price	$275	$150[c]

[a] The domestic markup is used to subsidize the cost of overseas marketing and education.

[b] The retail markup in overseas markets is determined by the local entrepreneur, but SUN OVENS suggests an approximate markup of 15–20%.

[c] If local materials are used, the retail price in overseas markets could come down to $100–115.

Organization

Leadership

Paul Munsen, President of SUN OVENS, entered the business ten years ago, originally as a favor to help the original inventor because the product at the time was causing a severe "financial headache." Coming from a background in business marketing, Paul admits:

> I knew absolutely nothing about solar cooking, didn't know what deforestation meant, and had no concept of anything when it came to the environment or the needs of the developing world.

However, this lack of knowledge actually serves Paul well in his current role. He believes one advantage of SUN OVENS is the fact that he is *not* an engineer and, hence, does not do business on what he calls a "product basis." According to Paul, all other solar oven makers are product-focused but SUN OVENS is "end-customer-focused" and, hence, SUN OVENS spends the bulk of its time and effort on marketing and education. While this hands-on effort with potential customers, often in very remote regions of the world, makes the company's efforts very difficult, it simultaneously enables its high impact when successful.

Culture and mission

After ten years, it is clear that Paul's dedication and tireless efforts are the company's main drivers — despite the numerous obstacles it has faced over the past decade. Indeed, Paul's presence can be felt throughout the small organization and, in many ways, SUN OVENS and Paul Munsen are so closely intertwined that it is difficult to separate the man from the company. This should be seen as a positive integration, yet this also poses potential organizational problems in the future (see "Organizational risk" on page 62).

A tour of the SUN OVENS facility in Elburn illustrates the simplicity of the design and manufacturing process, and illuminates the firm's commitment to meeting its environmental/social goals. A trip through the warehouse reveals a bevy of boxes of clothing, canned food, and other small items waiting to be shipped to developing countries. These items have been donated but have yet to be distributed to poor communities around the world. Paul explains this situation accordingly:

> Since SUN OVENS has to pay for the shipping container anyway to send its ovens overseas, any unused space within the shipping container is excess capacity that might as well be used for a good purpose. Thus, why not send some much-needed clothing or food items to those same remote customers.

Legal structure

SUN OVENS International is a for-profit corporation. Although admittedly many of its competitors are nonprofits, SUN OVENS was deliberately incorporated by Paul Munsen in 1998 as a for-profit enterprise because he believes companies selling truly valuable products that reduce poverty must be financially sustainable. If they are not, there is little incentive to scale and continue the product and its impacts long-term. In his own words, "it would be hypocritical to ask others to be profitable when SUN OVENS is not."

Organizational structure

Paul describes his organization as "very small and informally structured." With only six full-time employees, most of whom are involved in manufacturing and assembly, SUN OVENS typically has less clearly defined roles and chains of command. Moreover, as a flat, non-hierarchical organization, Paul is forced to take on multiple roles at any given time. These roles may include chief executive, accountant, supply chain manager, and sales person.

Processes and metrics

SUN OVENS tracks the environmental impacts of its products downstream (i.e., for its end-customers). It specifically tracks the carbon emissions and wood not burned as a result of the use of its ovens. Avoided wood results in fewer carbon emissions as well as higher-density forestation, and, if the fuel source is charcoal, emitted carbon dioxide (CO_2) and airborne pollutants will also be reduced. Notably, within each country in which it operates, SUN OVENS also tracks the time savings as well as financial savings from not having to harvest and/or purchase fuel for cooking.

One such example is in Haiti, where 99% of the Haitian countryside is now so deforested that wood is no longer a viable fuel source and families may spend as much as 50% of their household income on charcoal for cooking. In addition to the health implications, this deforestation contributes a whole host of other environmental problems ranging from topsoil erosion, silted streams, mudslides, and flooding. Solar-powered ovens can reduce acrid smoke from cooking fires by up to 70%.[12]

Another example of the impact of SUN OVENS® is their use in addressing HIV/AIDS in South Africa. Not only has the use of the VILLAGER SUN OVEN® provided employment for women with HIV/AIDS, but, by partnering with local bakeries that see the impact of reducing HIV/AIDS, SUN OVENS can combine the use of its product with bakers fortifying bread with additional nutrients to make the uptake of anti-retroviral drugs by weak HIV/AIDS patients much more effective. Furthermore, because 25% of the cost of bread is consumed by the energy needed for cooking, the savings resulting from the use of the solar ovens has allowed these HIV/AIDS-afflicted women to put 25% of gross sales into a fund that can be used collectively for other community development purposes.

12 "Science Hero: Paul Munsen — Solar Oven Man"; www.sunoven.com/international/
benefits.php, accessed April 20, 2009.

In general, SUN OVENS insists that a family of six using a GLOBAL SUN OVEN® for 80% of their cooking needs would save 4,800 pounds of wood per year. A GLOBAL SUN OVEN® has a useful life of at least 20 years; the wood saved by each oven would be 96 tons over its life-cycle. This would translate into more than 88 tons of avoided CO_2 emissions.

SUN OVENS does not track its own environmental performance or those of its suppliers.

Innovation

Subsidizing poor customers from the revenues of wealthier customers

SUN OVENS' dual-market business model of serving both wealthy customers and impoverished customers suggests strong potential for long-term viability. Using the higher profit margins from wealthy consumers to help offset the lower profit margins from poor consumers can be a very sustainable strategy. Indeed, several other hybrid organizations (e.g., Aravind Eye Hospital) use a similar business tactic in order to meet both their environmental/social objectives as well as their profit objectives.

It seems likely that, if SUN OVENS' long-term liabilities are paid in full, catering its products to both high-end and low-end customers could bring the company fully back into the black very quickly. However, the likelihood of these high-end markets continuing to remain viable in the long-term is still unknown.

Design for imitation while protecting your competitive edge

Every element of the SUN OVENS® design is meant to be replicable in developing countries and, hence, the design has remained simple since the founding of the company. The only part that is not replicable is the rubber gasket, which must be shipped from SUN OVENS. This proprietary gasket apparently allows food gases to escape but not the escape of air and water vapor. The fact that the gasket design is proprietary to SUN OVENS prevents others from being able to copy its design. All other materials (plastic housing, fiberglass insulation, aluminum reflectors, and wood paneling) are available in varying quantities in developing countries.

Even the assembly line in Elburn, IL, is very simplistic. As mentioned previously, while the workers in Elburn may use air-powered electric screw guns, if electricity goes out (which it often does in target-market countries), the screws can always be attached using a manual screwdriver. Similarly, the dies and fixtures used in Elburn are made of wood, or in some cases plastic, which allow for easy replication with whatever materials are available in-country.

Turning product demonstration into product down payment

Microfinance solutions are becoming increasingly common to help under-developed societies gain access to loans for new business ventures, or for new products and services directly. SUN OVENS has taken this model one step further by combining microfinance with product promotions and community education, thereby allowing potential customers to not only see the benefit of solar ovens, but also use the avoided fuel expenses towards the down payment of a GLOBAL SUN OVEN®.

Here's how the process works. SUN OVENS runs three-day demonstrations in Haiti to educate and teach women how to make and use simple cardboard solar ovens. On the first day of the training, participants are cooked meals using a GLOBAL SUN OVEN®. On the last day of the training, the participants cook their meals themselves with their homemade solar cooker. In between, attendees learn how a solar oven can cook meals much faster than traditional cooking methods. In addition, attendees are trained how to log their savings from reduced charcoal purchases, which are the source of energy for their traditional methods of cooking. Once the attendees understand the benefit of saving money, they are given the option of putting this saving towards the purchase of a GLOBAL SUN OVEN®. This enables a win–win situation for all involved in the process: the women learn the benefit of solar cooking and saving money, and SUN OVENS manages to increase sales.

Managing non–traditional challenges to meet mission objectives

Being in the business of selling products to the poorest of the poor, what some call the "Base of the Pyramid," is no easy task.[13] There are certainly

13 Base of the Pyramid, or BoP, consumers commonly refers to the billions of people living below the poverty line in developing countries.

many small and large enterprises looking to capitalize on the consumption possibilities of the global poor, yet it is clear that, in the case of SUN OVENS, being aware of non-traditional risks, i.e., those risks typically not faced by pure profit-oriented organizations, is a necessity for long-term viability.

One example of a non-traditional risk comes in the form of understanding the purchasing motivations of impoverished consumers. While understanding consumption habits and motivations is vital for every vendor of goods and services, the specific target market of the world's poorest people make understanding these drivers of consumption more difficult, and ultimately more risky. Part of this risk comes from the fact that access to these often remote consumers varies depending on local infrastructure, political sensitivity, and understanding of local customs. No market research is readily available, and statistical observations are either impossible to obtain or largely irrelevant. Thus, SUN OVENS must spend a considerable amount of time on field research and consumer education in order to make a sale, or partner with organizations that are trying to access those same markets.

In addition, in many poor communities, where desolation is so prominent and hope often lacking, product performance can be a big risk; if a product fails once, it is often not given a second chance. Unlike in developed countries, where product performance is often backed by guarantees or warrantees, such backup services are often incomprehensible or unfeasible in poor remote communities — if they are even desired in the first place. By focusing on addressing the cultural and legacy barriers first-hand, rather than through product specifications or other top-down approaches, Paul has shown that non-traditional challenges can still be turned into market opportunity.

Challenges for the future

Market risk

SUN OVENS faces multiple business risks — in both developed- and developing-country markets — in order to achieve long-term viability.

Developed–country markets

In well-established economies, SUN OVENS products are primarily purchased by green consumers and a handful of food enthusiasts. Numerous recent natural disasters in the U.S., in particular, have created a growing market in emergency preparedness. However, SUN OVENS has recognized that the simplistic design (wood paneling and "boxiness"), useful for production in developing countries, is not attractive to most developed-country consumers, or big-box retailers. Therefore, growing sales in developed countries will require a significant investment in design and manufacturing at the U.S. plant. But, by increasing stock-keeping units (SKUs), product complexity, and vendor customization of its products, SUN OVENS risks losing the economies of scale and access to consumers in developing-country markets.

Developing–country markets

This market is complex and full of potential barriers to market adoption of SUN OVENS' products:

- **Entrepreneurial financial risk**: since SUN OVENS has control over the early part of the entire value chain of oven delivery, there is considerable risk that the local entrepreneur will not be able to raise enough capital to meet the requirements of SUN OVENS contracts. This results in lost time and resources spent during the due diligence process. In addition, even if the contract is signed, there is still considerable financial risk if the entrepreneur cannot generate enough revenue within the local country to support the business

- **Import tax and customs risk**: there is often a considerable markup on foreign goods coming into developing countries. Not only can the cost of these import taxes completely undermine the business viability of solar oven projects, but an inability to obtain proper certifications and approvals can completely ruin projects already in progress.[14] This type of risk limits the geogra-

14 One illustration of this risk occurred when some American entrepreneurs wanted to open an eco-village in the Dominican Republic (DR). However, these entrepreneurs did not fully understand what was necessary to obtain all of the permits from DR customs. Accordingly, when the ovens arrived in-country, they were unable to get access immediately to the units. After much governmental wrangling, the entre-

phies in which SUN OVENS can operate. For example, India would be a particularly attractive market for solar ovens, but, due to incredibly high import tax and value-added tax (upwards of 50–100% of product cost), selling SUN OVENS® in India is simply too costly to be viable at this time

- **Cultural and/or gender risk**: the risk from being unable to convince women (who are the primary cookers in developing countries) to switch to solar ovens is often the biggest obstacle for solar ovens adoption. The fact that cooking is highly traditional means that these women are very reluctant to change. The additional challenge of dealing with customers who are largely uneducated (do not always understand the value of long-term budgeting), often near-sighted (focusing on survival day to day) and often risk-averse (if a product fails once, it must be bad) means that education and product demonstration is a heavy burden for SUN OVENS. In addition, local entrepreneurs are often male and their inability to relate to, communicate with, or even understand traditional cooking techniques creates additional cultural barriers to adoption

- **Legacy risk:** many people and programs have tried to introduce solar ovens to poor families in developing countries, but, because of poor quality (e.g., cardboard-based models) or an inability to keep food warm, such efforts have been known to lead to product backlash — sometimes resulting in physical abuse of wives (for serving cold food)

- **Geopolitical risk**: the fact that political strife can completely undermine projects in the pipeline creates immense volatility to SUN OVENS' potential revenue stream. Recent examples include projects in Kenya and Pakistan, which were expected to contribute more than $100,000 of revenue to SUN OVENS in 2008, but are indefinitely on hold

---

preneurs decided to move operations into a "Zona Franca" (free trade zone) within the DR, but, to this day, the entrepreneurs still have problems since they can get the ovens into the Zona Franca but still have challenges with DR customs to get them out.

Organizational risk

Perhaps the biggest risk to the long-term viability of SUN OVENS is Paul Munsen himself. Like many other organizations with committed, passionate, and tireless leaders, the success of the company lies on Paul's shoulders. With little evidence of succession planning in sight, Paul's retirement from the company could be a huge detriment to its future success. Although it is uncertain when this will come to pass, for the sake of the company, it is hoped that it will not occur anywhere in the near future.

Financial risk

There have been several investors interested in taking over SUN OVENS and rebuilding it after taking it into receivership. Chapter 7 and Chapter 11 bankruptcy are viable options, and Paul has stated that several investors have indeed offered to move the company into bankruptcy, take the intellectual property, and restart the company from scratch.

Paul admits that such activity would be cheaper than trying to pay off the numerous outstanding loans, but Paul remains true to the mission of the organization. He believes it is morally wrong and inconsistent to go bankrupt to escape the creditors, and he suggested the mission to assist others extends beyond developing countries. Paul strongly believes he can bring the company back into the black and he believes that the company is "so close" to a turnaround.[15]

However, these new investors are also interested in the overall mission of the company. According to Paul, "This kind of business attracts investors who want to make a difference and invest in a self-sustaining operation." Current investors (other than Paul himself) wrote off their investment a long time ago and no longer expect a return on their investment. They are totally passive, and thus allow Paul to act as the sole proprietor of SUN OVENS. These investors are all friends of Paul's and thus their patience and willingness to take a write-down is understandable in this situation. Paul insists that he intends to provide these investors with a return in the near future.

15 Personal communication with P. Munsen, Elburn, IL, January 18, 2008.

6

CASE STUDY
Guayakí — creating an entirely new value chain

Introduction

Chris Mann is not your typical CEO. At first glance one might mistake him for a California surfer with his long blond hair, untucked shirt, and friendly, easy-going personality. However, spend some time with Chris and one finds him to be exceptionally sharp and a shrewd business-man. His company, Guayakí (Gwy-uh-KEE), headquartered in Sebastopol, California, can be similarly misperceived. Guayakí is a small but growing beverage company that specializes in selling organic, rainforest-grown, fair trade yerba mate — a South American caffeinated plant which, when steeped in hot water, creates an infusion that provides a healthy alterna-tive to coffee or tea.[1] See Table 13 for an overview of the company.

---

1 Yerba mate is similar to tea in that it is made by steeping dried leaves of a plant. However, the leaves for tea and mate are obtained from different plants.

TABLE 13 Guayakí overview

Guayakí in 2008	
Annual revenue:	$7.3 million
No. of employees:	34
Headquarters:	Sebastopol, CA, U.S.
Environmental focus:	• Sustainable food/agriculture • Sustainable housing • Fair traded commodities
Profitability level:	Near break–even

Mission

Guayakí works directly with growers to deliver unique and beneficial products that enhance personal health and well-being. Our goal is to create economic models that drive reforestation while employing a living wage.

While, to many, it may seem that Guayakí is just another natural herbal drink company trying to ride the wave of organic and health foods being sold in the United States, this hybrid organization has a unique strategy for sourcing and selling its product. Over the past decade Guayakí has succeeded by using an innovative business model it calls "market-driven restoration." By purchasing Guayakí yerba mate, customers help support reforestation of the South American Atlantic Forest and improve the economic conditions of the farmers and indigenous communities that supply Guayakí.

Guayakí is not a company that merely pays lip service to the triple-bottom-line approach (i.e., measuring a company on its financial, social, and environmental performance); rather, its whole business model depends on it.

Early grassroots efforts by its founders have shaped Guayakí's success. They created a high-quality, premium product with a true social and environmental mission, and convinced other like-minded people to buy it. Today, however, Guayakí's creative marketing is using the health, energy, and weight-loss benefits of mate to reach a larger market. As a result, more players, including coffee and tea companies, are beginning to sell mate.

As the demand for mate grows, the Guayakí business model will be tested:

1. Can they hold onto their market share?

2. Will their suppliers be able to keep up with demand or are there limits to growth rate using this model?

Despite the uncertain outcome, one thing is clear: Guayakí's commitment to market-driven restoration will differentiate it from its competitors just as much as the laid-back nature of the company's CEO differentiates him from others.

Overview and history

What is yerba mate?

Yerba mate is a small tree native to the South American subtropical Atlantic forests of Paraguay, Argentina, and Brazil. South America's indigenous peoples have long used yerba mate leaves and stems to create a beverage they call mate, which they drink to boost and sustain their energy, health, and well-being.

Millions of South Americans consume mate daily as a staple of their diet. Deemed the "drink of the gods," mate is said to carry the same stimulant rewards of coffee or chocolate but with better health benefits, including clarity of mind, increased energy, and balance in body. According to the Guayakí website:[2]

> Yerba mate is nature's most balanced stimulant and naturally contains 24 vitamins and minerals, 15 amino acids, abundant antioxidants and naturally occurring caffeine.

A compilation of research published in the November 2007 issue of the *Journal of Food Science* supports these health claims and details yerba mate's health attributes and its potential benefit as a weight management drink (Heck and de Mieja 2007).

2   "All About Mate," guayaki.com/index.php?p=mate, accessed January 29, 2009.

How Guayakí mate is grown

High-quality yerba mate is shade-grown under the canopy of the Atlantic rainforest. The shade creates optimal conditions for growing thick and dark green mate leaves, distinguished by their lush, waxy finish. According to Guayakí, the tree's growth is carefully monitored:

> In the wild, the tree needs about 25 years to develop completely, reaching a height of up to 15 meters. When cultivated, the mate trees are pruned to a height of three to five meters to allow for harvesting. The harvesting (or careful pruning) of the leaves and tender stems begins after three to four years of age. Harvest takes place annually between May and July in most regions. At maturity, yerba mate has a unique bittersweet flavor. The tree can produce for about 40 years making it a perfect crop when sustainably harvested.[3]

These lush, shade-grown leaves contain more flavor and nutritional properties than thinner, sun-grown, commercial varieties. The challenge for growing mate in its native environment is the destruction of the Atlantic rainforest, more than 90% of which has been cut down for lumber, cattle grazing, and mono-crop agriculture.

How Guayakí mate is processed

The leaves and stems of mate are picked during harvest time in May, June, and July. Guayakí's harvesters follow organic certification guidelines, and weigh and label the leaves accordingly. From harvest, the leaves are transported to a mate processing center where they are dried by flash heating. Flash heating halts the oxidation process, keeps the dry leaves green, and preserves mate's nutritional properties. The leaves then go through either a wood-drying process that gives mate a smoky flavor, or an air-drying process that results in a lighter, "greener," flavor. The mate is then aged in a cedar chamber for 12 months. Prior to export, the mate is milled down to Guayakí's loose tea cut.

The traditional way to drink mate — a ritual and ceremonial process

Mate is traditionally shared with a group of friends or relatives and serves as a symbol of hospitality and connection for the group. Mate is tradition-

3 *Ibid.*

ally drunk from a gourd with a metal straw called a *bombilla* (see Fig. 15).

FIGURE 15 Gourd with *bombilla*

Tradition also dictates the way mate is to be prepared and served. One member of the group acts as the *cebador/a*,[4] the mate server, who prepares the mate by steeping dry leaves of yerba mate in hot (not boiling) water. This person drinks the first couple of mate gourds to ensure correct consistency and, once ready, refills the gourd with water and passes it counter-clockwise with the *bombilla* facing the recipient. When exchanging the gourd, eye contact is maintained between the *cebador/a* and the recipient, and usually no words are spoken. Saying "thank you" indicates that you do not wish to have any more. Each person takes as much time as they need to drink all the liquid from the gourd. Once finished, the recipient returns the gourd to the *cebador/a* in the same manner it was given, *bombilla* facing the person receiving the gourd. The *cebador/a* refills the gourd with hot water and passes it to the next person in the circle. This process continues until the mate is flat. Meanwhile active conversation is shared among the group.

Company background

Beginnings

Alex Pryor and David Karr founded Guayakí when they were seniors at California Polytechnic State University in San Luis Obispo, California, in

---

4 In Spanish, *cebador* denotes a male mate server and *cebadora* denotes a female mate server.

1996. Alex, from Argentina, and David, from California, became friends when they met at a local lunch spot. Being from Argentina, "where yerba mate has 95% market penetration (and toilet paper has 98%)," Alex loved to drink mate and introduced it to David over lunch.[5] After sharing a daily traditional mate gourd for a few months, David's lifelong allergies began to subside and he felt increased mental clarity and physical energy.

David became convinced of what Alex had been saying all along, that mate was a drink that should be brought to the United States. David left his computer business and started working with Alex to formalize the idea behind Guayakí. They soon generated a new restorative business model which would do three things. First, it would protect the South American rainforests. Second, it would provide needed income to the indigenous South American forest communities. Third, their plan would bring a healthy energy beverage to North America.

To move the venture forward, Alex and David brought Chris Mann, Michael Newton, and Steve Karr on board. Chris brought management and financial experience, Steven had graphic design expertise, and Michael was their salesman. These five made up the founding seed group. Together they traveled in a recreation vehicle, which they had decorated with a rainforest mural, while serving mate to any customers they could generate.

Between 1996 and 2007, they turned a small struggling mate company into an award-winning, rapidly growing consumer foods company.[6] Throughout this time, they demonstrated how hybrid organizations can be socially and environmentally driven while at the same time increasingly profitable.

Where they source their mate

Guayakí sources all its mate from the Atlantic rainforest. In the beginning, all was sourced from families who lived and worked in the Guayakí Rainforest Preserve in eastern Paraguay. Established by Alex's extended family in 1996, this reserve was where Guayakí's first yerba mate grew. After learning how to grow mate under the forest canopy in its native and lush

---

5 Personal communication with C. Mann, Sebastopol, CA, January 31, 2008.
6 Awards include the 2002 Green Business Award, 2004 Best Vegetarian Coffee Award, and 2004 Socially Responsible Business Award. For details, see www.guayaki.com/index.php?p=about&id=968 (accessed January 29, 2009).

environment, Alex trained the local people how to clear the right plants and maintain the forest in a sustainable manner.

However, in 2008 only 10% of their yerba mate comes from 34 families (approximately 200 individuals) who live and work in the Guayakí Rainforest and 90% comes from reforestation projects in Argentina and Brazil. In Argentina, Guayakí works with small family farmers and, in Brazil, it works with a family farm and two co-operatives.

Mate sourcing prices

In the early 1990s, Argentina attempted to stimulate economic activity by subsidizing mate. Supply became larger than demand and the market price of mate fell. Finding it difficult to survive on such low margins, mate-producing families began to convert their mate farms to cattle ranches or to monoculture crops. On behalf of Guayakí, Alex started meeting with farmers and offered to pay them two to three times the market price if they continued to grow mate. (This continues in 2008. The market price is approximately $0.75 per kilogram and Guayakí pays $1.80–3.00 per kilogram.) In addition, with bank financing and credit cards, Guayakí provided no-interest loans to help farmers begin pre-harvest operations.

Although Guayakí paid these farmers for all their crops, it would not use their mate until it met Guayakí quality standards. By showing local farmers how to create a higher-quality sustainable product and by giving them the economic motivation to do so, Guayakí has created personal and long-lasting relationships with its supply chain.

Using the Guayakí name — the Paraguay project

The name Guayakí honors the Aché Guayakí people. The indigenous Aché people are the last hunters and gatherers that remain in the Atlantic Forest. Via the company's Paraguay Project, Guayakí is working with the Aché people to grow mate and preserve their rainforest home. To do so, in 2002, Guayakí started a 20-year plan with the Aché people to grow mate. Guayakí trained a few Aché people to lead the project as managers and donated seeds for them to get started.

Guayakí has been paying the Aché a nominal fee of about $5,000 per year up until the mate is ready for harvest. When Guayakí reaches sales of $10 million (which its projects for 2008), it will pay 0.05% of revenues to the Aché people every year for use of the Guayakí name, as well as purchase all of the yerba mate they grow at two times the market rate.

Goals and objectives

Guayakí strives towards market-driven restoration — restoring the forests of South America, while at the same time providing a living wage to the indigenous people and bringing a healthy, organic energy drink to North America. According to Richard Bruehl, Guayakí's Vice President of Operations:

> Currently Guayakí holds 60% of the [U.S.] market and we don't see that lasting forever. Today the yerba mate market is a $15 million market and we hope it grows to a multi-billion-dollar market where we hold 10%.[7]

Reaching that goal will take more restorative work and an increased integration of mate into the North American culture.

Product information

Guayakí sells organic, fair trade yerba mate in:

- Mate tea bags — seven currently available varieties include Traditional, Pure Empower Mint, Chai Spice, Mate Chocolatté, Greener Green Team, Pure Endurance, and Pure Heart
- Loose mate
- Mate latte concentrates
- Mate gourds and *bombillas*
- Bottled iced mate drinks

Its best-selling products are its 25-count traditional tea bags and its eight-ounce loose bag. In addition, Guayakí yerba mate is used in the energy drinks Steaz and Sambazon Amazon Energy. Overall, Guayakí has about 20 SKUs (a few more include duplicate labels for products sold in Canada). Bottled drinks account for 45% of their overall sales, while dry products make up 50% and accessories the remaining 5%.

Guayakí has a warehouse at its company headquarters in Sebastopol, CA, where it stores most of its dried product and packs mate for the Canadian market. Outside co-packers pack the dried mate for the U.S. market, while bottlers on the East and West Coast bottle the Guayakí cold bever-

7 Personal communication with R. Bruehl, Sebastopol, CA, January 31, 2008.

age. Guayakí's products can be purchased at thousands of natural food stores, cafes and supermarkets throughout North America.

Business strategy and model

Guayakí market

While Guayakí sources its mate from South America, it primarily sells it to the North American market — the United States and Canada. International orders are accepted but make up only 1% of Guayakí's overall sales. Figure 16 illustrates how the company's strategic positioning has changed since its formation in 1996.

FIGURE 16 Guayakí's strategic positioning

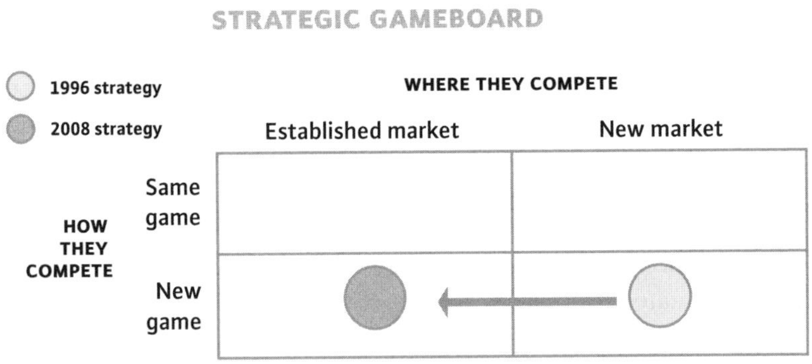

Within North America, Guayakí's target market comprises coffee, tea and energy drink consumers. Specifically, Guayakí targets its product to two subsets of energy drink consumers:

1. The health-conscious consumer (90%)

2. The environmental and culturally conscious consumer (10%)

The health-conscious consumer

Much of the Guayakí marketing material emphasizes the energy, health, and weight-loss benefits of mate. Among the health benefits listed on its website are induced mental clarity, sustained energy levels, weight control support, and bad breath reduction.[8] Chris Mann estimates that up to 90% of its customers purchase mate for these health reasons. In Southern California, where many residents are health-conscious, the cold bottled Guayakí drinks are the top-selling bottled tea-like beverages in natural food stores. Many of the consumers in this category may not be aware or even care about the social and environmental benefits that come with their purchase. The company believes that for most customers, even if they are aware of the social and environmental benefits, these benefits are not the primary reason for purchase.

Environmental and culturally conscious consumer

A smaller percentage of their target consumers buy Guayakí primarily for the positive social and environmental impacts. Chris estimates that 10% of consumers are compelled to purchase Guayakí because of its important mission, in addition to the other benefits that come with the product.

While the ultimate goal of Guayakí is a triple-bottom-line effect, another high priority is to expand this native drink throughout North America. Richard Bruehl, VP of Operations, says Guayakí has been very deliberate in its marketing efforts. When talking with consumers, employees must know what aspect of the product to pitch. The fact that Guayakí has many different angles from which to do so makes it more competitive. Guayakí can talk about many aspects of its products — they are organic, fair trade, environmentally beneficial, and a healthy stimulant. This combination of benefits creates a unique advantage that is helping Guayakí gain market share in a well-established beverage industry.

Distribution channels

Guayakí sells its product through three different distribution channels:

- Direct distributors
- Direct to wholesaler and partnerships
- Direct to consumer

---

8 "All about Mate"; guayaki.com/index.php?p=mate, accessed January 30, 2009.

Direct distributors

Direct distributors make up approximately 80% of Guayakí's sales. Through large national distributors such as United National Foods, a U.S. distributor certified to handle organic products, Guayakí products are delivered to thousands of natural food and chain grocery stores across the country such as Whole Foods, Wild Oats, Krogers, Safeway, and Vons. In addition, Guayakí uses smaller distributors for direct store distribution (DSD), i.e., to deliver, stock, and display Guayakí products in grocery stores. These micro-distributors typically focus on Guayakí's bottled products.

Direct to wholesaler and partnerships

Sales direct to wholesaler and partnerships comprise 10% of Guayakí's total sales. Wholesalers include coffee shops, cafes, and bookstores.

Guayakí partnered with Tully's Coffee Corporation in January 2007. In this exclusive partnership, Tully's features Guayakí's yerba mate in a series of beverages including brewed yerba mate tea, yerba mate lattes, mochas, shakes, and smoothies. Tully's was the first major specialty coffee company to carry the entire line of Guayakí products.

Guayakí has also partnered with Steaz Organic Energy and Sambazon Amazon Energy drinks by providing yerba mate as one of drink's main ingredients.

Direct to consumer

Guayakí makes 10% of its sales from direct to consumer orders. Of these orders, 70% come from the internet and 30% come by phone. Growth has been steady over the past few years.

In addition to web and phone orders, Guayakí recently opened a Mate Bar in the same building as its headquarters in Sebastopol, CA. The idea came from customers who had emailed suggestions. Guayakí management believes that the bar will generate enough money to break even; if it proves successful, there could be Mate Bars opening up around the country.

Business model

As mentioned earlier, Guayakí's innovative business model sets it apart from other beverage companies. While other companies may promote fair trade or organic practices, Guayakí is able to market that its product provides social, environmental, and health benefits.

Guayakí has pioneered a unique model called Market Driven Restoration (see Fig. 17). This model uses market forces to connect North American consumers with indigenous South American communities engaged in reforestation and sustainable agriculture in the rainforests of Argentina, Brazil, and Paraguay. The specific aspects of this triple-bottom-line approach are outlined below.

FIGURE 17 Guayakí's Market Driven Reforestation logo

Environmental stewardship

By teaching sustainable agricultural practices to indigenous South American farmers, Guayakí is contributing to the reforestation of the Atlantic Forest. This not only promotes carbon sequestration but also converts carbon dioxide to life-sustaining oxygen. In addition, forests contribute to a host of incalculable natural benefits and ecosystem services, including clean air, clean water, food provision, medicine sourcing, and building materials. By insisting on having the best-quality mate that is rainforest-grown, Guayakí is providing economic reasons for reforesting the Atlantic Forest and is showing the local citizens that the forest is much more valuable standing than it is cut down.

Social justice

By creating a premium market for rainforest-grown yerba mate and paying above-market rates for the product, Guayakí is supporting local cultures while providing a living wage. Unlike other companies, Guayakí does not simply broker its product; its Latin American team works with the local community to identify and respond to their needs. Because of these close relationships, the farmers put extra effort into the product and give Guayakí the best-quality mate. It is a mutually beneficial relationship.[9]

Economic viability

Guayakí exemplifies the fact that a company can be both profitable and adhere to a triple-bottom-line model approach. Guayakí internalizes the additional costs of fair trade and organic certification into its business model and allows customers who value these ideals to make a statement with their purchasing power. In addition, its business model demands a premium product and, accordingly, a premium pricing strategy. As its marketing tactics continue to tap into the growing market created by the desire of North American consumers to improve their health and well-being, Guayakí has been able to capture customers unaware of its entire three-pronged model. As consumers pay a premium for quality, they participate in driving social and environmental change.

Competition

Guayakí's main competitor is Eco Teas, an Oregon-based company that specializes in yerba mate. Eco Teas holds 30% of the total mate market. Its one-pound bulk bag of loose mate is its number one selling product, as it is for Guayakí, but it is listed at half of Guayakí's price. While Eco Teas' mate is organic, it is not rainforest-grown. In Guayakí's opinion, it does not offer the same quality. Like Guayakí, however, Eco Teas works with family farms in Argentina to supply the mate. Its operation is much smaller.

Other competitors in the organic, natural product space include Republic of Tea, Choice Teas and Yogi. Larger, more mainstream competitors include those that make high-fructose corn syrup drinks whose products include soft drinks, juices, and energy drinks. For example, Snapple and SoBe provide competition for Guayakí's cold bottled yerba mate beverage. In the organic and natural food space, Guayakí competes by marketing the fact that mate is a fair trade product and is organically grown in

9 Chris Mann says they calculate a living wage as follows: "We calculate it using a local basket of goods and audit. We also ensure that social security and healthcare are provided."

the rainforest. In the mainstream market, the health and stimulant benefits of mate are the larger focus.

As the company continues to grow, and as more competitors start to enter the mate market, Guayakí's business model will undoubtedly be tested. Chris Mann postulates that most entering competitors will come with organic, sun-grown mate. "It won't be rainforest-grown."

Because mate does not currently grow anywhere else in the world except in South America and needs specific conditions to grow, Guayakí may have a competitive advantage over new entrants provided consumers truly care about, and can differentiate, the rainforest-grown quality its brand offers. The relationships formed with so many local farmers and the premium brand that it has created gives Guayakí an edge that will be hard to imitate.

Headquarters relocation

For nine years Guayakí was headquartered in the city where it all began, San Luis Obispo (SLO), in the central coast of California. However, market saturation and a limited labor pool (Chris Mann cites difficulty in recruiting executive-level management to SLO) made Guayakí rethink its headquarters' location. Thus, the company decided to move to Sebastopol, California, in the northern part of the Bay Area. This is a region that has yet to reach mate saturation and enables more convenient air travel.

There were trade-offs to this decision. Northern California is slightly more expensive than SLO, so the cost of living for Guayakí employees has increased. However, approximately two-thirds of its SLO employees made the move. While the Guayakí executive team earns below-market salary rates for the area, they felt the move was important to the health and longevity of the business. As one of the biggest businesses in Sebastopol, Guayakí is already making a positive impact on the local community.

Finance

Sales and revenue

In 2007, Guayakí's revenues reached approximately $7.3 million, and, while they were operationally profitable, the company posted a modest loss when including interest, taxes, depreciation, and amortization. This loss is largely due to new placement costs and the launch of Guayakí's ready-to-drink bottled beverages. Sales are currently up 50% over last year's numbers and the company is on target to reach a breakeven in 2008 on sales of $11.8 million.

In 2007 Guayakí hired six employees, mostly as sales representatives, to help with its growth, but are hoping to stop hiring as it has begun to reach a critical mass in operations. While Guayakí has been profitable at various times in the organization's history, the past four years of operation has resulted in losses as it has been heavily investing in growth. Guayakí expects to become profitable in 2008 with its current level of staffing and past year investments.

Ownership structure

Guayakí began its business with eight shareholders. Alex Pryor, David Karr, Chris Mann, Michael Newton, and Steven Karr make up the five founding seed members and initially held a 95% stake in the company. The other three shareholders, their attorney and two friends, held the remaining 5%. Guayakí 's primary source of early-stage financing was through Small Business Administration (SBA) loans from a local San Luis Obispo bank and through leveraged credit cards with low-interest "teaser" rates (usually below 5%), which required constant balance transfers.[10]

In 2001, after a few years of hard work and grassroots efforts to spread the Guayakí brand name, the company was able to raise capital from outside investors. These included members of the Social Venture Network and local San Luis Obispo investors. These investors were all like-minded individuals who focused on using the power of business to create positive social and environmental impacts.

The first round of investments in 2001–2002 included approximately $100,000 from friends and family, and $350,000 from socially progressive venture capital funds. These funds were created by Ben & Jerry's, and include the Barred Rock Fund, which is led by Chuck Lacy (a Guayakí board member), and Hot Fudge Ventures, which was formerly run by Pierre Ferrari, Guayakí's VP of Marketing and Sales.[11] Pierre says patient

10 In 1997, Guayakí received a $50,000 SBA; in 1998, it was given another $100,000, and, in 2000, another $205,000. It also utilized $100,000 in credit cards between Chris, David, and Steven.

11 Other board members include John O'Shaughnessy, General Manager of Blue Diamond Growers.

equity from such investors has allowed Guayakí to present the return on investment as a composite of financial, environmental, and social values.

As of February 2008, the company had between 30 and 40 different investors with the seed group of five owning approximately 60% of the firm and other employees owning approximately 20%.

Venture capital interest and financing growth

After having been approached several times, management has considered selling Guayakí to external investors. However, they are not selling, nor selling out, anytime soon. According to Chris:

> It would be easy to sell Guayakí, but VCs [venture capitalists] want control. It would be difficult to maintain our mission if we only have 30% or 40% control. The beverage category is a lottery culture. We are competing in the market of Vitamin Water[s] [Vitamin Water sold to Coca-Cola for $4 billion]. Vitamin Water was not profitable at $80 million in sales, but kept raising capital. We could do the same thing, but realistically we can't grow that fast. If we wanted to grow from $8 million to $30 million in sales we would need $20 million in inventory and this is a constraint.[12]

From an operational perspective it is impossible for Guayakí to scale up the production of mate in a short amount of time, even if it wanted to grow its mission and double production. Key constraints include:

- Amount of lead time required to grow certified organic mate

- Time it takes to build relationships with local farmers and teach them the sustainable practices of growing mate for purposes of restoring the Atlantic Forest. Only a century ago, most of the Atlantic Forest was intact. Today, less than 5% of this forest remains

Chris estimated that it would take at the least 18 months to scale up in terms of quantity of mate needed, and noted that such growth would be difficult to enact while maintaining the high product quality.

For now, Guayakí hopes for steady growth of mate demand within North America. It will continue to finance this growth through traditional

12 Personal communication with C. Mann, Sebastopol, CA, January 31, 2008.

market-rate debt and patient equity investments, as well as reinvestment of its operating profits.

Organization

Leadership

Chris Mann, CEO of Guayakí,[13] was one of the five original seed members. His journey to Guayakí has been an unconventional one. After growing up in southern California, Chris attended Harvard University where he played football and earned an economics degree in 1991. He worked at Bank of New York for a few years after graduation and then relocated to Monterey, California, to head up the bank's mortgage branch. Although learning a lot while working at the bank, he soon became dissatisfied with the motivations of modern corporations, thus prompting him to quit his job and join a high school friend and now VP of Operations at Guayakí, Richard Bruehl, in starting a vegetarian restaurant in San Luis Obispo. From there, Chris met Alex and David, and subsequently joined Guayakí as the company's CEO. Chris was appointed CEO because of his finance and prior business background, and because he had the interest.

As described in the introduction, Chris is not a typical CEO. His unassuming and humble demeanor matches his leadership style, which his fellow management describe as "servant, leading by serving others, rather than others serving the leader," emphasizing collaboration and trust.[14]

Chris described the organization as operating with consensus-based leadership. Nothing in Guayakí is done without full consideration given to the environmental and social goals of the organization.

Recent additions to Guayakí include Patrick Lee, a former Balance Bar senior vice president, who joined in 2005, and Pierre Ferrari, a former senior vice president for Coca-Cola USA, who joined the team in 2007. Their roles are Global Cebador and VP of Sales and Marketing, respectively. These veteran industry leaders have been brought in to help manage Guayakí's growth.

---

13 Chris Mann's business card actually reads "Chairman of the Gourd."
14 From Guayakí's survey response for this study.

Structure

Guayakí is organized by functional departments; 34 employees are divided into six departments:

- Executive team
- Sales
- Marketing
- North American operations
- Latin American department
- Finance

While the organization chart (see Figs. 18 and 19) denotes hierarchy, management describes the operating structure to be highly collaborative and democratic.

The glue that holds the organization together is the Latin American team, which is composed of five people. Alex Pryor leads the Latin American team, which is based in Buenos Aires. This team maintains personal relationships with farmers in Argentina, Brazil, and Paraguay to ensure high-quality raw materials are produced for the company. They utilize six to eight different projects to yield a couple of hundred tons of yerba mate. Maintaining these relationships and having a geographically local Latin American team is a key component to Guayakí's competitive success.

Pierre Ferrari, Guayakí's Vice President of Sales and Marketing, suggests that its organizational structure helps the company meet its environmental sustainability goals. "All of our decisions," he notes, "are mission centered, which explicitly includes social and environmental stewardship of our whole supply chain."[15]

Culture and mission

Guayakí's mission statement is as follows:

> Guayakí works directly with growers to deliver unique and beneficial products that enhance personal health and well-being. Our goal is to create economic models that drive reforestation while employing a living wage.[16]

15 Online survey comments from P. Ferrari, November 4, 2007.
16 www.guayaki.com/index.php?p=faq&id=117, accessed March 11, 2008.

FIGURE 18 Guayakí executive team chart

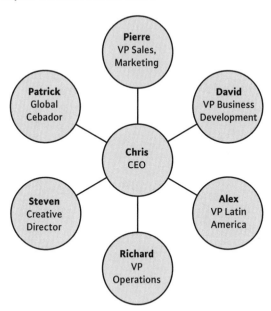

Guayakí's mission is completely embedded within the company culture. As Chris Mann explains, "The culture of mate is to celebrate the
human spirit. We had this mission before we had the sales, [thus] the
spirit is infused within our company culture."[17] To give an example, Chris
spoke about the company's meeting style. Every month, employees con-
vene in a large meeting space where they sit on the floor with pillows and
pass around gourds of mate, following the traditional ceremonial style.
Teammates are encouraged to spend the first part of the meeting sharing
personal as well as work issues. "Sharing out of the same vessel breaks
down barriers and is a real unifier for the employees," explains Chris. "It
keeps everyone connected."[18]

In addition to these types of non-traditional meeting styles, Guayakí
also offers some standard corporate benefits such as flexible work time
and 401k options for all U.S. employees. But, because of limited profitability, only 84% of its employees are paid at or above a living-wage salary for
the area. Guayakí is unable to pay full market salary wages to its executive team members. In addition, it provides insurance for each employee
but cannot offer it to all employee spouses or family members.

17 Personal communication with C. Mann, Sebastopol, CA, January 31, 2008.
18 *Ibid.*

FIGURE 19 Guayakí organization chart

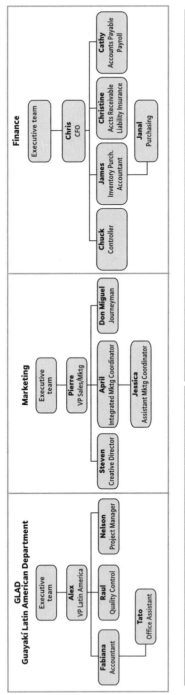

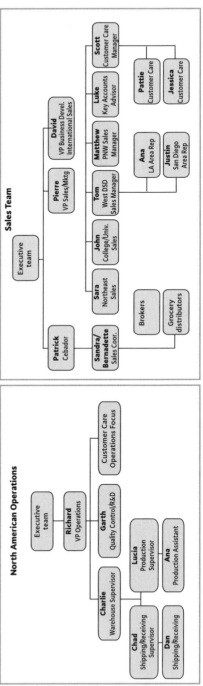

While Guayakí cannot provide all the typical benefits of a large corporation, the culture helps to maintain loyal employees. In 2007, World-Blue recognized Guayakí for dedication to democracy in the workplace. Employees completed a survey evaluating their company's democratic principles such as decentralization, accountability, and choice and integrity on a leadership level. Guayakí was one of 35 companies to receive the honor. To be a part of something that is greater than themselves is important to Guayakí employees.

Processes and metrics

Guayakí has many processes for ensuring the quality and sustainability of its products. It tracks environmental and social impacts upstream (i.e., from its suppliers), downstream (i.e., for its end-customers), and internally through its own operations.

Upstream

From an upstream operations perspective, Guayakí tracks the sustainability of its products from social, environmental, and quality perspectives. Socially, Guayakí is helping to support families across Argentina, Brazil, and Paraguay in maintaining decent livelihoods.

From an environmental perspective, Guayakí is helping to reforest the Atlantic Forest and maintain the rainforest's biodiversity. According to Guayakí's website:

> The Atlantic Forest of North Eastern Paraguay, North Eastern Argentina and Southern Eastern Brazil, is one of the world's top five biodiversity hotspots . . . and one of South America's highest priority sites for bird conservation . . . The 12,500-acre Itabo Rainforest Preserve [in eastern Paraguay] is home to over 330 species of birds and 36 species of mammals . . . Guayakí's project [in the Itabo Preserve] has also been singled out by the United Nations and other environmental organizations as one of the best examples of medium-scale sustainable agriculture use in South America.[19]

19 www.guayaki.com/index.php?p=reforestation, accessed January 30, 2009.

With regard to quality, Guayakí goes beyond standard food regulations to ensure its mate is of extremely high quality. Quality control specialists in South America and the U.S. test products against a comprehensive list of specifications. Guayakí has created its own checklist of guidelines which covers the supply chain from water source and soil to finished product. As Richard Bruehl remarks, "We want to be known as the greatest mate in the world. To get that gold standard we have to stay ahead of the curve."[20]

Downstream

For the end-consumers, Guayakí tracks both health and environmental impacts. As noted above, the leaves of yerba mate contain 24 vitamins and minerals, 15 amino acids, abundant antioxidants, and naturally occurring caffeine. For its end-consumers, yerba mate is touted as a healthy stimulant with a plethora of benefits, including clarity of mind, vitality, sustained energy, and well-being. In addition to positive health impacts, Guayakí has quantified the environmental impact of a consumer drinking a Guayakí product by suggesting that, "With two servings per day, a consumer helps protect approximately one acre of rainforest every year."[21]

Internal operations

Internally, Guayakí is dedicated to tracking its sustainability metrics. The company measures its ecological footprint for each product line — bottles and tea bags. Two examples of the company's dedication are its energy use and packaging.

Guayakí conducted an energy usage inventory and found that it was responsible for generating an estimated 28.5 tons of carbon dioxide annually. To offset its carbon emissions, the company buys solar power renewable energy credits from the Solar Living Institute in Hopland, California.

The company has also conducted a life-cycle analysis to demonstrate the net carbon dioxide emissions, subtracting sequestration, that result from its sustainable business practices. This analysis has shown that Guayakí's activities in South America offset over 100 tons of carbon dioxide. Thus, purchasing offsets are not needed to achieve neutral emissions and is instead built into the business model.

20 Personal communication with R. Bruehl, Sebastopol, CA, January 31, 2008.
21 www.guayaki.com , accessed 11 March, 2008.

All the boxes used for Guayakí tea bags are printed on 100% recycled paper with at least 55% verified post-consumer waste. In addition, all the company's tea bags are biodegradable. The company has recently started to use a biodegradable and home-compostable cellulose-based "biobag" to package some of its loose tea products.

Upcoming sustainability report and B Corporation status

Guayakí is making further efforts to be true to its triple-bottom-line mission. In 2007, it hired an independent third-party organization called Conscious Brands to collect data and write its first ever sustainability report, which was completed in 2008.

In addition, Guayakí is an official founding B Corporation. B Corporations are companies that meet exacting standards for environmental and social performance. A nonprofit organization called B Lab founded the B Corporation concept and certification process. According to its website:

> The mission of B Lab is to support B Corporations and this emerging sector by 1) certifying and rating B Corporations through the B Ratings System; 2) developing and disseminating a legal framework to institutionalize stakeholder interests within existing corporate law; 3) recruiting and promoting B Corporations; and 4) helping B Corporations access purpose-driven capital markets.[22]

To qualify for B Corporation status, companies must complete a survey of questions related to their environmental and social performance. Those that score 80 points out of 200 are usually included. In 2007, Guayakí scored 110 out of 200 in the survey and were awarded B Corporation status.

22 www.bcorporation.net/index.cfm/fuseaction/content.page/nodeID/08c9dc4d-6064-48cb-af04-4fd9d4ced055, accessed May 28, 2009.

Innovation

Raw materials pricing/sourcing based on market-driven restoration model

Guayakí is most proud of its innovative triple-bottom-line business model, designed to bring mate to North America while simultaneously creating economic demand that supports reforestation and provides a living wage. The business model is as sustainable as the yerba mate tree itself. As long as demand for the product stays constant or increases in North America, local growers will be paid a premium to practice sustainable agriculture and contribute to the reforestation of their environment.

Guayakí's business model shows that profitable business can result from an environmental and social mission. Such innovative thinking can be an inspiration to all business leaders seeking to create positive social and environmental impact.

Infusing mate into the North American culture

Guayakí has been able to adapt a traditional bitter-tasting drink to the modern needs of the Western world. Appealing to the health-conscious habits of Americans has enabled Guayakí to compete with the coffee and tea industry. In the process they have formed a new beverage category for yerba mate as a healthy stimulant beverage. In addition, the creation of various mate flavors (and Guayakí's innovative extract, e.g., the greener green tea, mate chocolatté and mate lattes), as well as its expansion into cold bottle beverages, have collectively allowed Guayakí to reach an even larger market.

While Guayakí's social and environmental missions are written all over its product packaging and marketing materials, the high quality of the product has driven its success. Guayakí has brought a staple Argentine product to North America and is converting it to satisfy multiple needs.

High-technology eco-package design

Guayakí pays close attention to detail in all aspects of its product and pushes environmental innovation. Its tea bags utilize "flow-through" technology to maximize brewing yield, flavor, and potency of the product.

In addition, these bags are made from eco-friendly filter paper, which is itself made of biodegradable unbleached hemp and wood pulp. The tea box utilizes all its panel space to communicate Guayakí's mission, along with the health and nutritional values of the product. As noted above, the box is also made of 100% recycled paper with at least 55% verified post-consumer waste.

Potential sale of carbon credits

Guayakí is always generating new ideas. Currently, it is investigating the possibility of selling its own carbon credits. Because its business model generates forest regrowth and forests sequester carbon, there is the possibility that Guayakí produces a net environmental benefit when it comes to its carbon footprint. If offsets are built into the model, Guayakí could potentially sell excess carbon through its website and use the funds to create new reforestation projects.

Challenges for the future

Defining a living wage

Guayakí's mission is to provide a living wage to the local farmers of South America who supply its product. However, Guayakí is unable as yet to provide a living wage to all of its Sebastopol employees. Only 84% make market or above-market salary rates ($16 per hour for Sebastopol, California). Executive employees earn below-market salary rates, which poses a challenge when they are living in a high-cost area such as northern California. Furthermore, while individual health insurance is provided for all, not every employee receives spouse or family healthcare coverage. If Guayakí wishes to keep its employees happy, it will need to find a way to meet their living wages. There is a clear tension between meeting the social needs of the South American farmers and meeting the needs of its corporate employees.

Managing growth rate and balancing market and mission

In February 2008, Guayakí sales were up 50% from the year before. While growth is good for the company, managing this growth is crucial. Creating relationships with the South American growers and teaching them the practices of sustainable agriculture takes time. Trying to grow too fast can jeopardize the quality of the product and the Guayakí mission. Thus, Guayakí will have to take care when balancing market demand and mission objectives.

Culture change

In 2007 Guayakí hired six new people, mostly in sales. While some of these hires were to make up for those employees that did not relocate with them to Sebastopol, some were hired to help manage growth. With growth comes the potential for culture change. Guayakí has a unique and tightly knit culture. This culture is vulnerable to dilution or collapse should Guayakí have a tremendous growth spurt. For example, how would the company be able to maintain its unique meeting style if the organization was to double in size? While doubling in size is not something that will happen anytime soon, Guayakí must be prepared for how it will manage culture should significant growth occur.

Changing consumer habits

Guayakí has found that it is extremely difficult to change people's habits. Indeed, it can take generations to do so. Bringing mate into a market that is dominated by coffee has been challenging. Getting people to try mate is the first step. According to Chris Mann, once they do, people frequently comment on how amazing mate is, and sometimes explain how it has changed their lives. The trick is to keep such customers coming back. Guayakí has learned that persistence and patience are vital. While it can take generations to change a habit and perhaps longer to change economics, Guayakí has already demonstrated that change is possible.

Educating consumers to combat competition

Guayakí's promotional materials state that its products are organic, rainforest-grown and fairly traded. For the average consumer, how do these practices measure up against another mate company whose product may be only organic? Will Guayakí's sustainable practices have negative financial consequences, as other competitors using sun-grown mate provide products that are more affordable for the average consumer? Educating consumers to understand and care about the difference will be crucial for Guayakí to combat its competition.

7

CASE STUDY
Eden Foods — lasting leadership and the risks of succession

Introduction

Succession planning can be difficult for any enterprise, especially with a strong, charismatic leader at the helm for many years. This is especially true for hybrid organizations where the mission and goals often contain aspects that are different than traditional enterprises. How an organization plans for a change in leadership is key to its continued success. With Eden Foods, Inc. of Clinton, MI, the problem of succession planning is at the forefront.

Eden Foods, Inc. is the oldest natural foods company in North America (see Table 14 for an overview of the company). It lives by the credo put forth by its founder and current president Michael Potter, "Still doing what we set out to do."[1] While all Eden Foods employees believe in the company's mission to provide the highest quality organic foods for the benefit of its customers, Michael's passion and consistency of message have contributed to the success of the company.

---

1 "Company Goals"; www.edenfoods.com/about/goals.php, accessed May 28, 2009.

TABLE 14 Eden Foods overview

Eden Foods, Inc. in 2008	
Year founded:	1968
Annual revenue:	$45 million
No. of employees:	116
Headquarters:	Clinton, MI, USA
Environmental focus:	• Clean air • Clean water • Sustainable food/agriculture
Profitability level:	0–5% profitability

Mission

Provide the highest-quality organic foods for the benefit of our customers.

The ideas and values Michael originally set forth still permeate everything Eden Foods does. Should Michael step down or leave unexpectedly, the culture and mission of Eden Foods would constitute the true succession planning at the company. By keeping the mission and goals of the organization simple and consistent, Eden Foods plans to continue as a successful hybrid organization for many years to come.

Overview and history

Industry overview: natural and organic foods

Organic foods have been the fastest-growing segment of the entire food industry, and have seen double-digit growth for each year between 1997 and 2007. The much larger U.S. natural and organic foods industry totaled over $28 billion in 2005. In 2006, sales of organics alone grew 20% and reached a total of over $16 billion. Packaged goods, in which Eden Foods primarily competes, made up over $2 billion in sales in 2006. Although the market for both organic and natural foods is large and growing, the value of Eden Foods' sales at $100 million constitutes a fairly small share of a much bigger market dominated by larger corporations.

FIGURE 20 Organic industry acquisitions

Source: Phil Howard, www.msu.edu/~howardp/organicindustry.html, accessed May 28, 2009.

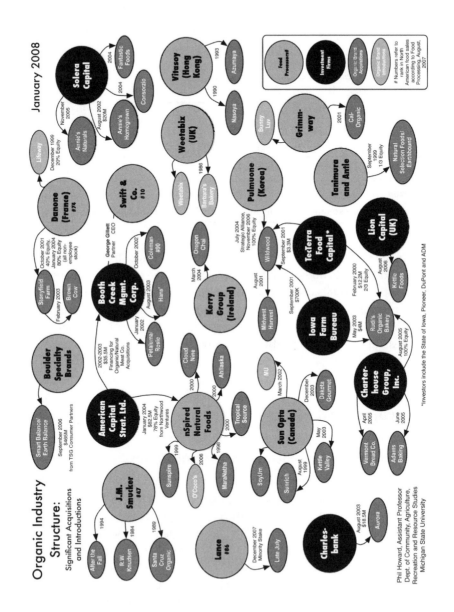

Consolidation within the natural and organic foods industry began as early as the 1970s and 1980s, and accelerated beginning in the early 1990s. Figure 20 illustrates this trend. This competition has been particularly challenging for Eden Foods. Silk® Soymilk, for example, was a relatively minor player in the field of soy drinks until it was bought and distributed by Dean Foods in 2002. This cut deeply into Eden's sales of soy products. The dominant position, large distribution networks, and deeper pockets of larger companies such as Dean Foods, Kraft Foods, Inc., and H.J. Heinz, will continue to be a challenge for smaller independent manufacturers like Eden Foods.

Background information

Eden Foods traces its beginnings back to 1968, when a small group of people motivated by the macrobiotic phenomenon attempted to find whole-grain vegetarian foods produced without chemicals.[2] This group started a co-op to purchase these products, which were unavailable in local grocery stores. The co-op evolved into a natural foods store and deli in Ann Arbor, MI, known as the Eden Deli.

As the customer base grew and began to ask for more products, the co-op evolved into a distributor of these types of foods in order to meet customers' needs. At about the same time, it changed its name to Eden Foods, Inc., and began a long-standing relationship with artisan Japanese food makers to import their products into the United States. The company began offering 100% certified organic grains, and then diversified into pasta, soy milk, and eventually into canned beans.

Today, Eden Foods functions as a primary supplier/manufacturer, carrying over 380 stock-keeping units (SKUs) including the Japanese foods, pasta, canned goods, snack foods, teas, and extracts. In 1980, Eden Foods closed its deli and store and moved 20 miles from Ann Arbor to Clinton, MI, where all products are currently supplied, primarily through customer pickup and a small fleet of six trucks. Eden also owns a warehouse and sales operation in San Francisco, CA. The company obtains many of its products from 325 local family farms and 60,000 acres of organic farm land (Eden Foods 2007).

---

2 A brief history of macrobiotics can be found on the Macrobiotic Guide website (macrobiotics.co.uk/history.htm, accessed May 28, 2009).

Goals and objectives

While the emphasis has changed over the years, Eden Foods' goals and objectives have stayed consistent throughout its 40-year history. Through its move to Clinton and its expansion to California, Eden Foods has stuck to its mission of supplying the highest-quality natural foods to its customers. As illustrated in Figure 21, Eden Foods pays particular attention to environmental, social, and economic factors through its products as well as its employees and suppliers. These goals permeate almost every decision made by Eden Foods. All employees — from top management to line workers — buy into these goals and the overall mission of Eden Foods.

FIGURE 21 Eden Foods goals

Source: Eden Foods, Inc., "Company Goals"; www.edenfoods.com/about/goals.php, accessed May 28, 2009

1. To provide the highest quality life supporting food and to disseminate accurate information about these foods, their uses and benefits.
2. To maintain a healthy, respectful, challenging, and rewarding environment for employees.
3. To cultivate sound relationships with other organizations and individuals who are like minded and involved in like pursuits.
4. To cultivate adaptability to change in economic, social, and environmental conditions, to allow Eden the opportunity to survive long term.
5. To have a strong, positive impact on farming practices and food processing techniques throughout the world.
6. To contribute to peaceful evolution on Earth.

Product information

While the two largest categories of products by sales are canned beans and Edensoy® soy products, representing 29% and 23% respectively, the company currently carries a wide variety of products (see Fig. 22).

The majority of its products are grown and sourced from the United States. The exceptions are various products from Japan, quinoa from Ecuador, sea salt from Europe, and olive oil from Spain.

The processing of the majority of the products occurs in North America. The pasta products are made in Detroit, MI, beans are canned in Eaton, IN, soy products in Saline, MI and Quebec, Canada, and some snack foods are in produced in Clinton, MI and packaged in Battle Creek, MI (see Fig. 23).

FIGURE 22 Eden Foods product categories

Source: Eden Foods, Inc. 2007

- Organic pasta
- Organic quinoa
- Soba and udon noodles
- Artesian spring water
- Organic Edensoy®
- Organic beans
- Organic Lundeberg SGB rice and beans
- Organic tomatoes
- Organic sauerkraut
- Organic malt sweetener
- Organic apple and cherry
- Oil and vinegar
- Condiments
- Imported traditional Japanese food
- Soy sauces, mirin, and ponzu
- Organic miso
- Japanese sea vegetables
- Imported tea and infusions
- Snacks, crackers, and chips
- Food concentrates and supplements
- Tooth and gum care
- Bulk beans, flour, and grains

Each of Eden Foods' processing plants is certified and rated "Superior" by the American Institute of Baking (AIB), ensuring the highest standards of production.[3] All of the organic products are certified by the Organic Crop Improvement Association (OCIA).[4] Eden Foods also maintains its own testing laboratory at its Clinton headquarters to ensure the quality of the ingredients.

Eden Foods is product-, not market-driven. New product ideas come from within the company. When an employee conceives of a product that they want to see on the shelves, they fill out a Product Merit Form, which is taken to Michael Potter for approval. When management approves the idea, a Feasibility Sheet is created to ensure that the product can be financially competitive. Then, a Product Development Team takes the idea to

3 More information and a history of AIB certification can be found at www.aibonline.org and in Wirtz 1994.

4 www.ocia.org

FIGURE 23 Map of Eden Foods locations

Source: Eden Foods, Inc. 2007

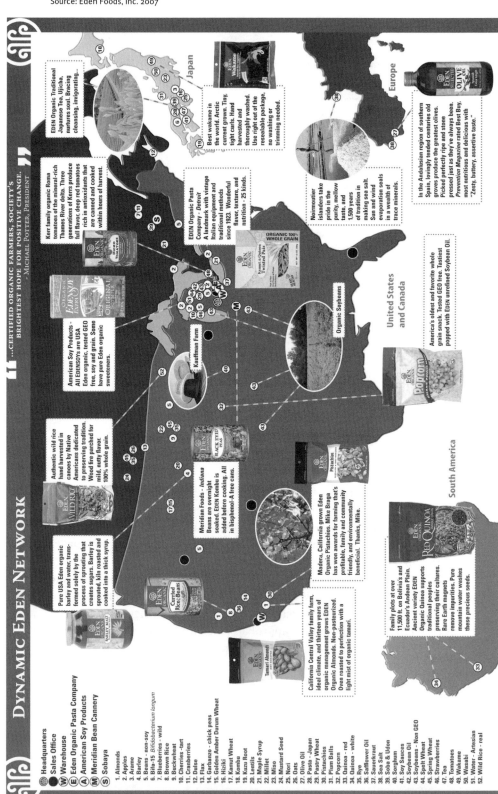

a test kitchen where samples and tasting occurs. Finally, table-top testing occurs with larger machinery and batches. During this stage, the recipe is adjusted to be suitable for large-scale production.

Business strategy and model

Strategy

Eden Foods competes in the traditional markets for organic foods both nationally and internationally, selling its products to major chain stores and smaller natural food outlets. As Figure 24 illustrates, Eden Foods began competing in a new market with new products.

FIGURE 24 Eden Foods' strategic positioning

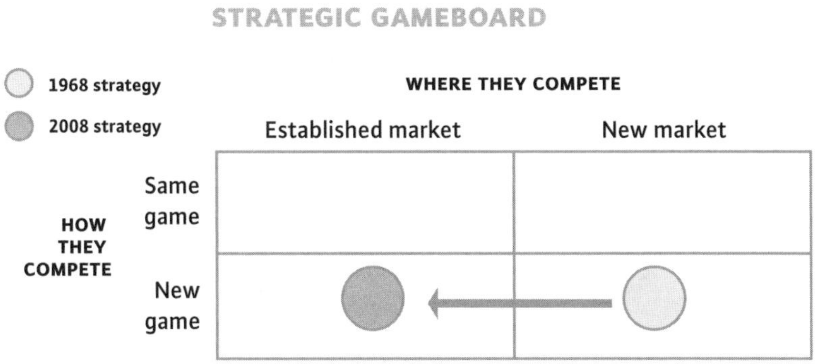

As the market matured and became established, Eden Foods continued to offer something different in its products. Its strategy has been to provide the highest-quality ingredients and supply innovative products. In this respect, the company is trying to work within this market, but create a niche in which these product attributes are especially valued. Given the cost structure of its raw materials, Eden Foods cannot normally compete on price with the larger corporations in this market, so its strategy revolves around having unique, high-quality products that consumers can trust.

Thus, the story behind the products is particularly important, because consumers need to understand the benefits of their quality. In order to do this, Sue Becker, Director and Vice President of Marketing and Sales, states, "We need to use the package to tell our story."[5] The packaging of Eden's pasta, which is color-coded to illustrate the whole-grain content and includes the health benefits of individual products, exemplifies this goal (see Fig. 25).

FIGURE 25 Examples of Eden Foods product packaging

Source: Eden Foods, Inc. 2007

Business model

Since its inception, Eden Foods has attempted to keep sourcing and production close to its headquarters in Clinton, MI. Thus, the company attempts to purchase products from nearby farms as much as possible. However, it has also learned to diversify the risk of localized crop failure by sourcing from multiple locations. Processing of the majority of its products takes place in Michigan, Indiana, and Quebec, Canada. The majority of its sales occur by customer pickup, so the company needs only a small fleet of trucks. Eden Foods sells its products to natural food stores throughout the country, and its soy milk can be found in most of the major supermarket chains.

5 Personal communication with S. Becker, Clinton, MI, January 11, 2008.

Quality control is a major aspect of the business model for Eden Foods. The company does not buy from farms that it has not previously visited. The company's procurement team usually visits the farms during spring and before harvest. Eden also has its own quality control lab at its headquarters. Established in 1998, this lab does testing for shelf-life, proteins, microbiology on all nuts and fruit products, as well as genetically modified organism (GMO) testing on rice and beans. Products are tested three times, once in a preliminary batch, again in a final batch, and finally as the finished product.

The company also has strong relationships with its producers. Many of the farmers come to Eden first to sell their products because of these relations. Eden Foods is also a part of several growers' groups, thus solidifying this relationship.

Competition

With the growth of the natural and organic food market, many of the larger food companies have entered the organics industry, and the competition has become very intense. This is particularly troubling for Eden Foods, as these larger companies have begun to limit the supply of raw materials, thus driving up the price. Also, such companies can charge lower prices for sometimes inferior products, making Eden Foods products seem much more expensive.

Finance

Sales and revenue

With annual sales of over $35 million in 2005 and 2006, Eden Foods has relatively stable revenue. The majority of sales are in the U.S. market, but the company also sells products in Canada, Australia, South and Central America, and the Middle East.

The market outlook for natural and organic foods continues to be favorable. According to the *Organic Trade Association's 2007 Manufacturer Survey* (OTA 2008), the industry will grow by 18% for each of the years between 2007 and 2010. With such large and sustained growth projected for the industry, Eden Foods can expect a continued stable revenue stream.

Liabilities and obligations

As shown in Figure 26, Eden Foods relies on traditional market-rate debt to finance its operations. As a mature organization, the company does not see the need to rely on alternative forms of financing. The company has traditionally worked with community banks for its financing needs, but as Jay Hughes, Director of Finance, states, "We have been with one community bank for a long time and this is the third time we have outgrown them."[6] Recently, Eden Foods began to talk to larger national banks, and, due to its financial strength, the company has found that financing is relatively easy. Given Eden Foods' location in the economically depressed area of southeast Michigan, many banks have been approaching the company with financing opportunities. The company also relies on roughly 20% of its financing through reinvestment of operating profits.

FIGURE 26 Funding sources for Eden Foods

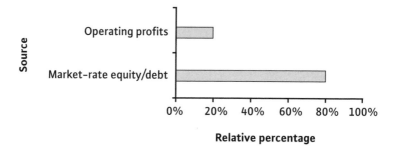

Eden Foods' financing structure has been particularly advantageous for the company and its environmental sustainability goals. Without having doubts about securing financing for its operation and not being beholden to a large number of shareholders, the company can provide a market for products from organic farmers. Eden Foods does not carry a heavy debt burden, further enhancing its ability to successfully achieve its goals.

6 Personal communication with J. Hughes, Clinton, MI, January 11, 2008.

Organization

Leadership

Eden Foods would not be the same without Michael Potter's leadership and vision. He has been running the company since he was 19 years old and is the unconditional leader of Eden Foods, as all decisions seem to go through him. This does not mean, however, that he does not share the leadership of the company with his employees. According to Sue Becker, "Michael's door is always open. He doesn't always agree, but is willing to take time to look at your idea."[7]

This concept is echoed throughout all levels of the organization. Bill Swaney, Director, Executive Vice President and General Manager, observes that, "As management, we pass down responsibility with confidence that they will do it. Employees have the freedom to be creative in the way that they choose."[8] This is an important aspect of the organization. While Michael is definitely the leader of the organization, he relies heavily on his top management, each of whom believes strongly in the organization's mission.

Mission and culture

Throughout the 40-year history of Eden Foods, the mission and culture of the company has remained consistent. The idea that the company's main purpose is to supply high-quality wholesome food to the public exemplifies its mission. This can be seen in its product-driven focus, wherein it only examines the market forces later in product development. The mission comes directly from Michael.

Many founders of natural and organic food companies have sold out to larger companies, but this is not the case with Eden Foods. As Jay states, "Michael will be here as long as he is alive and the mission will never change."[9] This continuity in leadership and mission has proven to be one of the key success factors for Eden Foods.

This does, however, represent a major risk to the organization. Without Michael, a possible leadership vacuum exists. Eden Foods attempts to mediate this risk by assuring that:

7 Personal communication with S. Becker, Clinton, MI, January 11, 2008.
8 Personal communication with B. Swaney, Clinton, MI, January 11, 2008.
9 Personal communication with J. Hughes, Clinton, MI, January 11, 2008.

1. The mission of the organization is clear and simple

2. All members of the organization buy into it

Legal structure

Eden Foods, Inc. is a for-profit organization incorporated in the state of Michigan as an S-Corporation, with Michael Potter as the sole shareholder. The company formed as a co-op, changed to a C-Corporation in 1969, and converted to an S-Corporation in 1992 through a reverse stock split. The conversion was done primarily for tax and estate planning reasons for Michael. Except for its beginning as a co-op, Eden Foods has always been a for-profit organization. Its commitment to the stewardship of the land and ties to local farmers are simply part of its mission as a corporation and no thought has been given to changing from its current legal structure.

The current structure places a lot of power into Michael's hands, and this only magnifies the risk of the organization losing its focus and mission if Michael can no longer fulfill his role. However, the company has a succession strategy in which the Board of Directors, consisting of top management, takes control of the company. As each of these members believes in the mission of the organization, the risk of Eden Foods losing its way is lessened.

Organizational structure

Michael describes his leadership style as "participative," where he openly shares decisions and authority with subordinates. This is reflected in the views of the rest of the organization. Despite being structured along traditional functional areas, the company maintains a flat structure with less clearly defined roles and chains of command. Ideas can come from anywhere in the company, but final authority rests with Michael. However, many employees echo the fact that his door is always open and he seems receptive to their ideas. Some employees describe the organization as very lean, with many people wearing different hats and taking on multiple roles. This is not unlike many other small and medium-sized businesses, as well as nonprofit organizations.

Employee satisfaction with the structure of the organization is reflected in an average of almost 17 years of employment of the top-management team, and this continuity contributes to the success of Eden Foods.

Processes and metrics

Eden Foods states that it tracks the environmental impact of its products upstream with its suppliers, through its company operations, and downstream through the product impacts.

The company tracks:

- Energy consumption

- Chemical usage

- Waste production

These factors are tracked through customized in-house tools. This tracking is, for the most part, informal and the exact metrics used are unclear. Moreover, no formal reporting is done. Bill Swaney stated that, while they would like to create a sustainability report in the future, there is no pressure to do so at this time.

The focus on sustainability is particularly intense on the supply side. According to Jon Solomon, Purchasing Department Manager:

> Eden is all about stewardship and responsibility, at least on the supply side. For example, another company focused on organics could purchase every certified organic item from China and it would be drenched in oil. Prices would be significantly less. Eden chooses not to do that because of our responsibility to support North American agriculture and organics. Our soy beans and other beans come out of Michigan. They're local. We have a great reputation and dedication to purchasing sustainable food.[10]

Sustainability is simply a part of the decision-making process of the company. While not all levels of the organization know about or understand the exact metrics used, everyone understands the environmental impact of the products, raw materials, and operations.

Sustainability is such an integral part of the mission and goals of the company that formalized tracking of environmental metrics is deemed unnecessary by the management.

10 Personal communication with J. Solomon, Clinton, MI, January 11, 2008.

Innovation

Eden Foods is proud of its innovative relationships with its suppliers. The company believes these relationships are unusual for its industry, and that the quality of the products and the ability to bring new products to market are reflected in its relationships.

Another innovation within the company is in product development. Being a product-driven company, Eden Foods relies on new ideas coming from all levels of the organization.

Working closely with suppliers

The most innovative aspect of Eden Foods, according to Michael Potter, is the personal relationships the company maintains with all its supplier farmers and their families. The company has numerous stories about how these relationships have led to highly profitable new products. The idea to can organic beans started from an excess of products from the farmers, leading Eden to look into a way of preserving the beans and ensuring that the farmers continued to sell the beans for an organic premium. This close relationship with growers has proven to be a competitive advantage for Eden Foods. The story behind its products also assists in its marketing and connection with consumers.

Product development

Anyone within the company can suggest new products. The product-driven nature of Eden Foods ensures that these suggestions can often turn into innovative new products. While the vetting of new products can be as rigorous in Eden Foods as any other organization, the proliferation of new ideas from throughout the organization can be a competitive advantage.

> Innovation comes from all parts of the organization because of our culture.[11]

---

11 Personal communication with B. Swaney, Clinton, MI, January 11, 2008.

Challenges for the future

Market risk

Two of the main market risks to Eden Foods are the consolidation of the natural and organic food industry, and the cost increases on all raw materials.

Consolidation of natural and organic food industry

Few independent producers of natural and organic foods remain. Many of these companies have been bought by private equity firms and larger corporations. This consolidation gives the larger companies an advantage in distributing and marketing their products, especially accounting for the tandem consolidation of the natural foods retail channels. While Eden Foods has a devoted client base, its cost and lack of widespread product distribution could hamper its growth prospects for the future.

Raw material cost increases

Across the board, raw material prices have shown unprecedented increases over the past few years. Increases in packaging costs, agricultural product costs, and energy prices have hurt Eden Foods, particularly given the company's emphasis on quality. Other companies can attempt to source cheaper materials, but Eden Foods' relationship with its suppliers and uncompromising attitude about sourcing quality products represent a significant risk for the future.

Organizational risk

The greatest organizational risk for Eden Foods relates to the succession of leadership when Michael Potter leaves the company. The loss of Michael would leave an incredible void in the company, one that could possibly lead to the end of the Eden Foods as it is now known. While the mission of the company can be counted on as a great strength, this mission is represented in the persona of Michael. Whereas a succession plan is in place for Eden Foods, his loss could shake the foundation of the company. The employees of the organization have a strong belief in the mission and goals set forth, and Michael has attempted to keep the mission and goals simple and consistent. However, this continues to represents the greatest risk to the organization.

8

CASE STUDY
Maggie's Organics — connecting producers and consumers to the cause

Introduction

As of 2008, Maggie's Organics, headquartered in Ypsilanti, MI, was the oldest organic apparel company in the United States (see Table 15 for an overview of the company). Holding itself to the highest standards of social and environmental responsibility, Maggie's Organics is dedicated to changing the way business is done in the apparel industry. The company was founded with the goal of saving land from the devastation of conventional cotton growing and, as a first-mover, it played an important role in the development of the U.S. organic cotton apparel industry.

One of Maggie's core values is that "there is no environmental sustainability without social responsibility."[1] Thus all products are made by workers in the U.S. and Latin America who have a safe working environment, fair wages, and an active voice in their future. The most celebrated

1 www.maggiesorganics.com/socialaspects.php, accessed May 28, 2009.

TABLE 15 Maggie's Organics overview

Maggie's Organics in 2008	
Year founded:	1992
Annual revenue:	Not available
No. of employees:	14
Headquarters:	Ypsilanti, MI, USA
Environmental focus:	Sustainable agriculture
Profitability level:	Consistently profitable since 2004

Mission

To produce and provide comfortable, durable, affordable, and beautiful articles of apparel and accessories made from materials that restore, sustain, and enhance the resources, including human, from which they are made.

example of this commitment is the 100% worker-owned co-operative in Nueva Vida, Nicaragua, with whom Maggie's has worked closely since 1999.

Having worked for organic food companies for several decades before founding Maggie's in 1992, Bená Burda, founder and President, is a pioneer of the organics industry. Her perspective on the mission-driven values of her company, she explains, is unique. "I am not a fair trade person, and I'm not socially responsible. This is simply the way we choose to do business and we wouldn't do it any other way."[2] The passion and dedication that she infuses into her business has resulted in deep, personal relationships with all the producers and many of Maggie's customers.

Bená and her team work hard to communicate the benefits of organic cotton to their producers and consumers alike. She believes that this connection to the company's mission contributes to the development of loyal and trusting relationships, which are the cornerstone of Maggie's financial, environmental, and social successes.

2 Personal communication with B. Burda, Ypsilanti, MI, January 24, 2008.

Overview and history

Industry overview: organic cotton apparel

The organic cotton apparel industry began in the U.S. in the early 1990s. Fueled by the eco-fashion trend of the early 1990s and demands from apparel companies such as Esprit and Levi's, who both introduced "eco" clothing lines, organic cotton farm acreage in the U.S. grew from 100 acres in 1989 to 25,000 acres in 1995.

But there were a variety of problems associated with this production expansion. First, organic cotton items were more expensive, and customers weren't willing to pay a premium for them. Second, companies had trouble telling the organic cotton "story" without discounting their conventional cotton items. In addition, the supply of organic cotton was volatile because the industry itself was so new. Moreover, the fashion industry went through a "retro" phase in the mid-1990s, which brought synthetics back into favor and caused the "eco" clothes trend to flounder. For all these reasons, the bottom fell out of the organic apparel market, many companies went out of business or stopped offering organic cotton lines, and, by 1996, U.S. organic cotton farming had dropped to 10,000 acres.

However, 1996 also marked the year that Patagonia made the decision to use only 100% organic cotton in its cotton clothing. This fueled

FIGURE 27 Estimated global retail sales, organic cotton products

Source: Organic Exchange 2006

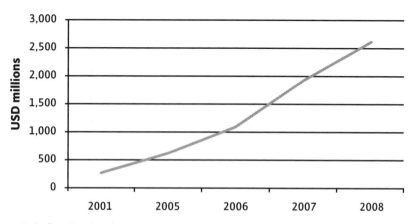

2008 sales figure is projected.

the renewed growth of the organic cotton apparel industry. Within a few years, Patagonia's efforts helped to significantly raise consumer awareness about the environmental and social value of organic cotton in the U.S. The industry saw tremendous growth from 2000 to 2008, in part due to long-term commitments by brands and retailers to use organic cotton, and in part because of overall consumer lifestyle changes towards sustainability. As Figure 27 shows, the estimated global retail sales of organic cotton products increased from $245 million in 2001 to $583 million in 2005, reflecting an annual average growth rate of 35%. By the end of 2008, sales were expected to reach close to $2 billion (Organic Exchange 2006).

Why choose organic cotton?

Conventionally grown cotton is one of most heavily sprayed field crops in the world, and conventional cotton growers typically use many of the most hazardous pesticides on the market. These include aldicarb, phorate, methamidophos, and endosulfan. Utilizing 2% of worldwide farmland, conventional cotton farming consumes 10% of the world's pesticides and 25% of all insecticides.[3]

Sprayed from the air, these highly toxic pesticides often drift over farmhouses, roads, water sources, and workers, contaminating water and soil, and creating health dangers for wildlife and humans. Because cotton is also a food crop, namely through cottonseed oil used in snack foods and in rations for beef cattle, pesticide-laced cotton that enters the food supply poses a global public health threat.

The threats of conventionally grown cotton are disproportionately distributed around the world; because 99% of all cotton farmers live in developing countries, the developing world bears the brunt of the environmental and health problems caused by conventional cotton production (EJF 2007).

In contrast, organically grown cotton prohibits the use of synthetic chemicals to control pests, except in extreme cases. Instead, natural predators and intercropping are used to control pests, and special machinery and fire control handle weeds (EJF 2007). A field must be pesticide-free for at least three years to be certified organic.

---

3 "Problems with Conventional Cotton Production," PANNA (Pesticide Action Network North America); www.panna.org/files/conventionalCotton.dv.html, accessed January 29, 2008.

Recognized organic fiber certifying organizations include Control Union World Group (formerly SKAL), OCIA International, and NASAA. All three organizations are accredited by the National Organic Program (NOP) of the U.S. Department of Agriculture (USDA), and this accreditation allows products certified by these organizations to be sold in the U.S. The NOP standards apply to organic agricultural production within the U.S. as well as to organic products being imported into the U.S.[4] These standards require field certification only, meaning that only the organic certification of the raw commodity (cotton or wool) is recognized in the U.S. and, as of 2008, there were no organic processing standards.

Background information

In 1992, Maggie's Organics was founded in Ann Arbor, MI by Bená Burda and her former business partner, Jennifer Mueller. By then, Bená had worked in the organic food industry for 14 years. Maggie's was the second organic apparel company founded in the U.S., and is the oldest organic apparel company remaining in the market as of 2008.[5] It is one of the few companies in the apparel industry that sells 100% organic clothing.

The idea for Maggie's started with an organic tortilla chip. In the early 1990s, Bená was working for an organic food company that was sourcing blue corn from Texas farms to produce tortilla chips. She noticed that some of the chips were faded in color, and asked a farmer for recommendations on how to improve the quality of the corn. He recommended rotating in organic cotton crops on the land that the blue corn was being grown. When his cotton produced a yield, the farmer asked Bená to help him sell it. Bená's business partner invested $500,000 into the organic cotton fiber before the company even had its first product. The first products — socks produced by North Carolina knitters — emerged soon thereafter.

Bená considered the socks a good first product because they were small and inexpensive "impulse" purchase items. These socks became one of the first non-food products sold at the Natural Food Expo in California.[6] This event not only marked the beginning of the company's growth,

---

4 "National Organic Program," U.S. Department of Agriculture; www.ams.usda.gov/nop/indexie.htm, accessed January 29, 2009.

5 A company called Eco-Sport was the first seller of organic cotton apparel in the U.S. but no longer exists.

6 The Natural Food Expo is now called the Natural Products Expo.

it also the highlighted one of the company's primary competitive advantages — selling organic apparel products at retail stores and trade shows dedicated to food products.

As of 2008, Maggie's Organics carried over 350 stock-keeping units (SKUs), and sold its products in over 1,500 stores across the United States.[7]

Goals and objectives

Maggie's Organics was founded with the intention of saving the planet's land from the devastation of conventional cotton growing. Since 1992, Maggie's Organics has manufactured apparel and accessories made from certified organic fibers (certified by Control Union World Group, OCIA International and NASAA) while utilizing fair labor practices. Maggie's mission is:

> To produce and provide comfortable, durable, affordable and beautiful articles of apparel and accessories made from materials that restore, sustain and enhance the resources, including human, from which they are made.[8]

Product information

Maggie's produces organic clothing in four major categories:

- Apparel (shirts and pants)
- Socks
- Tights
- Baby wear

As of 2008, most of the apparel and baby wear was produced at 100% worker-owned co-operatives in Nicaragua and Costa Rica, while the socks were produced by knitters in North Carolina, and the tights were produced in Peru.

All Maggie's products are made from certified organic fibers. These are primarily cotton, but several varieties of socks are made from organic

7 Approximately 75–85% of these stores are conventional or natural food product stores.
8 www.maggiesorganics.com/maggiesstory.php, accessed May 28, 2009.

wool. Most of the products contain small percentages of other materials, primarily nylon, Lycra®, and rubber. Doug Wilson, Bená's husband and the Vice President of Sales, describes Maggie's as a "blue collar" organic company, meaning that, while a small organic premium is included in the price, they work hard to keep prices low and refuse to take advantage of the consumer.[9,10]

Business strategy and model

Strategy

Maggie's competes in the U.S. market for organic cotton apparel, selling its products both to major chain stores and to smaller "mom and pop" retailers. When it was founded in 1992, Maggie's was competing in a new market with new products (see Fig. 28). As the organic cotton apparel market matured and established itself, Maggie's maintained its competitive advantage by continuing to sell exclusively organic apparel products

FIGURE 28　Maggie's Organics' strategic positioning

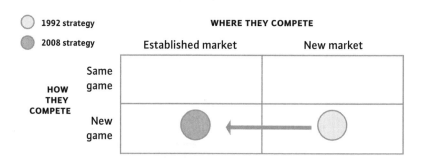

9　Personal communication with D. Wilson, Ypsilanti, MI, January 24, 2008.
10　Organic cotton is more expensive to produce than regular cotton for two primary reasons: (1) due to the crop rotation system, one-third of the cash crop is out of production every year; (2) lack of synthetic fertilizers results in a 20% lower yield (Ecomall 2008).

and distributing its products through the large U.S. natural *food* distributors.

Bená's intention when starting Maggie's was to establish a new norm for the way a successful business could be operated within the apparel industry, which she accomplished by creating a business that respected the environment and the lives of the people making the products.

Sourcing

In the beginning, the company sourced cotton primarily from U.S. farmers. Supply was readily available and this strategy aligned with the company's mission to purchase fiber from the closest possible source, thereby reducing the energy required to transport it to Maggie's production facilities. But, as the industry evolved and as demand for organic cotton increased, it became more difficult for Maggie's to source only within the U.S.

As of 2008, Maggie's organic cotton is purchased from a number of different countries worldwide; though as of 2008, its supplies came primarily from Turkey, and were subsequently shipped to the production facilities in the U.S., Nicaragua, Costa Rica, and Peru.[11]

The company chooses not to source cotton from China or India, due to the comparatively high energy costs required to transport the cotton to Maggie's production facilities, as well as the questionable labor practices sanctioned by the governments of these countries. The company is dedicated to being a leader in a sustainable and responsible industry, and the management team believes it is important to source from the most credible suppliers possible.

In addition to making sure that all of the cotton used for production is certified organic, Maggie's abides by the Organic Trade Association (OTA)'s American Organic Standards for Fiber Processing.[12]

Production

In the 1990s, Maggie's production facilities were also exclusively U.S.-based, including contractors in Alabama, Tennessee, North Carolina, and California. Between 1999 and 2000, Maggie's lost five cut-and-sew house

11 Turkey produced the most organic cotton globally in the 2006/2007 growing season: "Frequently Asked Questions," Organic Exchange; www.organicexchange.org/faq2.php, accessed January 29, 2009.
12 www.maggiesorganics.com/standards.php, accessed May 28, 2009.

contracts to bankruptcy, and Bená became increasingly frustrated with quality control problems and the inability of the remaining contractors to meet deadlines. When she visited these facilities, she discovered that the "women producers were literally indentured servants." Most, she observed, were undereducated single parents who had absolutely no incentive to produce high-quality goods.

Bená's dissatisfaction with the production options in the U.S., and the fact that many producers started to go out of business, led her to consider offshore options, but she would only go ahead with this plan if she could be completely sure that Maggie's clothing was not produced under unethical sweatshop conditions.

In 1999, Peter Murray, Maggie's Production Manager, met Michael Woodard, the Director of the Center for Development of Central America, a non-profit organization located in Managua, Nicaragua, at an organic meeting in the U.S. Michael was trying to help Nicaraguan communities recover from the devastation caused by Hurricane Mitch in October 1998, which destroyed their homes and left many individuals living in refugee camps. Unemployment was one of the biggest problems Michael saw, so he and his team decided to explore models of worker-owned co-operatives. The Production Manager asked Michael if any of these people knew how to sew, and Michael said that with 40,000 people working in sweatshops in Nicaragua, some of the people in the refugee camps would surely know how to sew. Bená believed this was the answer to Maggie's production dilemma and told Michael, "if you can build this, we will come." She promised that, if Michael could get the co-operative off the ground, Maggie's would give it as many apparel sewing contracts as they had left in the U.S.[13]

This was the genesis of a 100% worker-owned sewing co-operative in the refugee community of Nueva Vida, Nicaragua, which today is known as The Fair Trade Zone (FTZ) Sewing Co-operative. This co-operative is the world's first 100% worker-owned free trade zone — a geographical area where some normal trade barriers, such as tariffs and quotas, are eliminated in hopes of attracting new business. Historically, multinational companies have used these zones to set up production factories in developing countries. The Fair Trade Zone co-operative's status as a free trade zone contributes to the co-op's economic success.

13 "Ants That Move Mountains," Maggie's Organics, Video, 2008; www.maggiesorganics. com/media/ants.wmv, accessed January 29, 2009.

Phish Food for thought

Bená describes a major turning point in the history and strategic direction of Maggie's — the "aha" moment — when she realized that it would be much easier to create high-quality products when the producer herself has a vested interest in the enterprise's success.

In 1997, Ben & Jerry's had just launched a new flavor of ice cream, Phish Food, in a joint venture with the eponymous band. Ben & Jerry's and Phish organized a benefit concert to mark the launch of the new ice cream flavor and to raise awareness about the increasing pollution of Lake Champlain. All the proceeds from the concert were designated to contribute to the restoration of Lake Champlain.

Ben & Jerry's was Maggie's biggest customer at the time, accounting for approximately 40% of Maggie's sales revenues and an average of 100,000 T-shirts per year. The ice cream company placed an order with Maggie's for 14,000 T-shirts, which had been designed especially for the benefit concert.

Days before the concert, the production facility owner called Bená and told her there was no way he could have the concert T-shirts ready on time. Bená, realizing that the future of her company was potentially at risk, drove her van from Michigan to the facility in Alabama. She joined the production assembly line and, when the owner told her to leave, she responded by telling him that she was not leaving until she got her T-shirts.

At first the women in the production facility looked at her like she was crazy and did not speak to her, but Bená began to talk to them about the importance of both the organic cotton that they were sewing, as well as the benefit concert for which the T-shirts were being made. For the first time, the women had a connection to both the material they were sewing and the end-customer and cause. Many of them called home and told their families they were going to be getting home late from work that day (and the rest of that week) because "they had a lake to save."

Bená personally delivered all 14,000 T-shirts to Burlington, VT, in time for the benefit concert, and came away from the experience realizing that in order to maintain the consistent, high-quality production required to ensure the future success of Maggie's, she needed to find an operation in which the producers had skin in the game through ownership and profit-sharing.

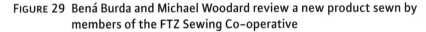

FIGURE 29 Bená Burda and Michael Woodard review a new product sewn by members of the FTZ Sewing Co-operative

The co-operative building was constructed by the women themselves, and, as of 2008, the co-operative was owned and operated by 65 women, who earned over 70% more than the average annual per capita income in Nicaragua. They work a regular Nicaraguan work week of 47 hours. Overtime is paid double and is completely voluntary. No workers are under the age of 18. Being a co-operative, the members decide collectively how they will be paid (hourly or by the piece, for example), what holidays to take, etc.

By contracting the sewing of its garments to the co-operative, Maggie's has made it possible for the women to create community sustainability in a highly impoverished area of Nicaragua. This partnership allows the women to take control of their own lives, set up a trust fund to support the development of other businesses in their community, and provide stable, livable income for their families.[14]

At the beginning of this partnership, there were growing pains as the women learned to sew to the specifications of Maggie's products. But they got up to speed quickly and were soon producing high-quality goods for

14 "Clothes for a Change — Leaders of the Apparel Industry," OCA (Organic Consumers Association); www.organicconsumers.org/clothes/leaders.cfm, accessed January 29, 2009.

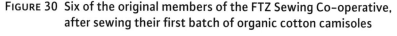

FIGURE 30 Six of the original members of the FTZ Sewing Co-operative, after sewing their first batch of organic cotton camisoles

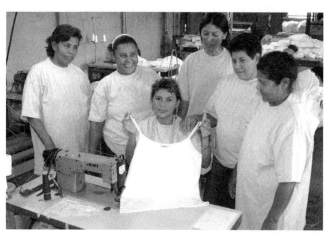

sale in the U.S. market. Beginning in 2007, some quality problems started to re-emerge and Bená believes these are a result of the women becoming more independent and less willing to listen to feedback from the Maggie's team.

Bená acknowledges that the partnership with the co-operative has, in some ways, stifled the growth of the company. From the beginning, Bená made a strong commitment to stick with them and she refuses to pull out, even if goods are not delivered by deadline or quality is not up to par.

Maggie's relationship with the FTZ co-operative is completely different than that which it had with its U.S. sewing contractors. With the U.S. contractors, the relationship was only with the management and Maggie's was simply one of several clients to them. In contrast, the company's contract and commitments to FTZ put the co-operative in business, and (for a long while) kept the co-operative in business. In addition, because the producers are the owners, the relationship with Maggie's extends to every member of the co-operative. The result is that Maggie's is more than just a client to FTZ.

Michael Woodard, who still plays an integral role in the operations of the co-operative, has said:

> The happiest and saddest day of my life will be when they tell me to go away — we don't need you anymore. I hope one day

they can internalize what they can verbalize so well — that they
own the co-operative, run it and benefit from its success.[15]

For Bená, there is a tension between wanting the women to reach their
full potential in terms of independence and self-sufficiency, and needing
them to receive and integrate constructive feedback from the Maggie's
production team to ensure high-quality products. There is a quality control process, and, if product standards are not met, the products are
either shipped back or deducted from the supplier's credit.

The management team believes it is important to treat the co-operative
like any other supplier and not cut them any slack in terms of quality.
Maggie's is dealing with the recent quality issues in the same way that it
has always approached its partners — with respect, transparency, and
communication — and as the company's track record has shown, these
tactics generally lead to successful outcomes.

Distribution

Maggie's sells its products exclusively in the U.S. via wholesale, retail, and
direct-to-consumer channels.

Wholesale channel

A large part of the Maggie's success story is based on the fact that it is
the only company selling certified organic cotton apparel through some
of the largest *food* distributors in the U.S. These distributors generate a
significant amount of revenue for Maggie's. Doug Wilson is very proud
of this achievement and hopes that the company is able to maintain its
position as the sole organic apparel company in this channel. In addition
to these large food distributors, Maggie's works with smaller distributors
and a brokerage firms, which act as sales representatives for its products
and other companies' products in the natural products industry.

Retail channel

Maggie's sells products directly to many independent natural food retailers. Doug takes pride in the solid relationships it has formed with these
"mom and pop" natural food stores across the U.S. and Canada.

---

15   "Ants That Move Mountains," Maggie's Organics, Video, 2008; www.maggiesorganics.
     com/media/ants.wmv, accessed January 29, 2009.

Direct-to-consumer channel

As of 2008, 8% of total sales revenues were generated from orders placed by consumers on the Maggie's website.[16] These orders are fulfilled and shipped from the Maggie's headquarters in Ypsilanti, MI.

Competition

The organic apparel industry has evolved into a fairly broad sector, with numerous companies making products with at least some amount of certified organic fibers. The industry includes retailer giants such as Nike (the largest T-shirt manufacturer in the U.S.), American Apparel, and Edun — Bono's (lead singer of the rock band U2) socially conscious apparel company. Organic clothing makes up only a portion of the apparel sales for each of these companies, and more importantly, these companies do not compete in the same market as Maggie's.

Because of the unique positioning that Maggie's has as an apparel company in the natural food market, the competition is relatively small, particularly in the smaller stores. The company faces its greatest competition in the national retail chains that sell a large collection of both natural foods and organic apparel — one competitor in this category is Whole Foods. But in many smaller retail stores that sell Maggie's products, no other organic apparel is sold.

Finance

Maggie's Organics was initially financed by Bená and her business partner, Jennifer Mueller. In 1997, Bená bought out the company from Jennifer by creating a parent company called Clean Clothes, Inc. As of 2008, the company was majority-owned by Bená, with two of her friends holding partial ownership.

The company has been consistently profitable since 2004. Over the years, Bená has utilized a very conservative fiscal approach and has been able to grow the company without taking in outside capital since a friend gave the initial $10,000 investment in 1997 to help start Clean Clothes, Inc.

16 www.maggiesorganics.com

The majority of the capital required to start Clean Clothes, Inc., as well as the capital required to buy out Jennifer's shares of Maggie's, was made available to Bená through a credit line she opened in 1997 using her own personal guarantee and resources as collateral. She periodically taps into that credit line, but has not needed to find outside resources to fund the company's growth.

As a privately held company, Maggie's has a policy of not sharing additional financial information with the public.

Organization

Leader-driven mission

Bená Burda's career in the organics industry began in 1978 when she dropped out of the University of Michigan to start working with Eden Foods. After ten years at Eden Foods, she took a position as a sales manager for Bearito's Brand Organic Tortilla Chips, and, as described earlier, the idea for the Maggie's business arose while seeking a natural solution for the problem of the fading color of the company's blue corn tortilla chips. Without any knowledge of the apparel industry, Bená took on the challenge of putting the inedible cotton crop to good use, and Maggie's was born.

When Maggie's was founded in 1992, there were no governmental standards for organic clothing, and, as of 2008, these standards still did not exist. But Bená used her leadership position on the Organic Trade Association's Fiber Council to formulate the American Organic Fiber Processing Standards, which are industry-led and apply to the U.S. and Canada. OTA's organic fiber processing standards, approved in January 2004, address all stages of textile processing, including post-harvest handling, wet processing (including bleaching, dyeing, printing), fabrication, product assembly, storage and transportation, pest management, and labeling finished products. They also include an extensive list of materials permitted for, or prohibited from, use in organic fiber processing under the standards.[17]

17 "Four industry leaders will be honored at All Things Organic," OTA (Organic Trade Association) press release, April 30, 2002; www.ota.com/news/press/29.html, accessed January 29, 2009.

The OTA standards have been incorporated into the Global Organic Textile Standard, an international, non-governmental collaboration that allows for a single organic-textile certification mark, accepted in markets worldwide. Sandra Marquardt, who co-ordinated OTA's Fiber Council steering committee, stated:

> Without [Bená's] drive, I doubt the organic fiber processing standards would have become part of the OTA American Organic Standards or the new Global Organic Textile Standards (Oliver 2007).

When the U.S. cut-and-sew production industry began to collapse in the late 1990s, Bená found an alternative to the sweatshops used to produce much of the conventional textiles sold in the United States.

Bená's passionate leadership has driven Maggie's to become a role model for the apparel industry in terms of commitment to socially and environmentally responsible sourcing and production practices. The Organic Trade Association recognized Bená's leadership role in the organics industry by choosing her to receive the 2002 Organic Leadership "Special Pioneer Award".[18]

Organizational structure and culture

Legal structure

Maggie's Organics is a brand of the parent company, Clean Clothes, Inc., and is a registered C-Corporation where Bená is the primary shareholder. Clean Clothes, Inc. is 90% owned by Bená and 10% owned by a friend who invested some of the start-up capital. The company has a board of directors, though it is rarely involved in the decision-making of the company.

While the company has very close relationships with several co-operatives in Central America, these organizations are wholly worker-owned and independent of Maggie's.

Organizational structure and culture

Maggie's is a very small company, with 14 employees working in its sole administrative office in Ypsilanti, MI. There is a warehouse in the Ypsilanti office and another in North Carolina. This small size is reflected in

18 *Ibid.*

the close-knit culture of the organization, as well as the strong relationships that the company has with all of its suppliers. Bená commented that, "developing relationships with people who work in the mills and sew our garments is one of the unique things about Maggie's."[19] While Maggie's operates within defined functional areas, in practice it is a notably flat structure, with a family atmosphere that extends beyond Bená and Doug's wife–husband management team.

The Maggie's office culture is built on a foundation of respect, which Bená and Doug strongly believe contributes to the company's success. The company pays competitive wages and there is a relatively small difference between the salaries of the lowest- and highest-paid employees, including Bená and Doug. The lowest-paid employee earns slightly more than 50% of the salary of the highest-paid employee. All employees receive full health insurance benefits, plus an additional $1,000 annual heath and wellness benefit to cover the cost of alternative medical treatments not covered by the traditional plan. Perhaps the most unique feature of the Maggie's benefits package is the free monthly massage available to each employee. "We hope that our employees feel good about working at Maggie's and therefore can be a part of the company's campaign," says Doug.[20]

Processes and metrics

Environmental processes and metrics

While Maggie's does not yet formally track its environmental sustainability performance, this is an important goal for Bená and Doug, and they plan to begin tracking when they can justify spending the resources.

Despite the lack of formal tracking processes, environmental sustainability is an integral part of the everyday decisions and strategies of the company. The company mission includes:

1. Raising awareness about the harmful impacts of conventional cotton

---

19   Personal communication with B. Burda, Ypsilanti, MI, January 24, 2008.
20   Personal communication with D. Wilson, Ypsilanti, MI, January 24, 2008.

2. Leading the way to a more sustainable and responsible industry and product

All the cotton and wool sourced for Maggie's products is 100% certified organic. For the post-harvest production process, Maggie's abides by the OTA's American Organic Standards for Fiber Processing — a set of standards that Bená played a major role in creating. The OTA standards are voluntary, and there is no official certification for companies that abide by them.

In addition to ensuring the environmental sustainability of the organic fibers from harvest to production, Maggie's also works with its printing and packaging partners to implement more sustainable procedures into their company operations. One success story on this front is VGKids — a screen printing company in Ypsilanti, MI. By working together, Maggie's has become the preferred organic cotton T-shirt supplier for all VGKids' customers. In addition, Maggie's was able to work directly with James Marks, owner of VGKids, to explore phthalate-free inks and other alternatives to conventional printing. These inks are now part of VGKids' standard procedures for all printing options.

Social process and metrics

Again, Maggie's does not formally track its social impact performance, but the labor standards used by the company are based on those of the internationally recognized grassroots anti-sweatshop organization, The Clean Clothes Campaign.[21]

Maggie's requires full disclosure of working conditions and production standards for each of its producer partners. A questionnaire for all suppliers — developed to ask specific questions about average salary, benefits, healthcare, etc. — is reviewed before production begins as well as on an annual basis. In most cases, a Maggie's employee visits the facilities and interviews workers, as well as management, to ensure that workers' rights and needs are respected.

As of 2008, there were no third-party audits of the production facility working conditions. Maggie's is working with the Fair Labeling Organization to develop third-party standards for auditing all stages of production, but this will take time to implement.

---

21 For more information, see www.cleanclothes.org. The Clean Clothes Campaign is not related to Maggie's Organics parent company, Clean Clothes, Inc.

Innovation

Pioneer of organic apparel industry

Maggie's is the oldest surviving organic apparel company in the U.S. It is one of the few companies in the apparel industry that offers clothing made with 100% certified organic cotton and maintains direct relationships with its manufacturers.[22] Guided by Bená's passionate leadership, Maggie's played a critical role in the development of the U.S. organic apparel industry and has remained a model for social and environmental stewardship within the industry. According to Doug, one of the key factors in Maggie's success is the growing numbers of "consumers with a conscience." Without them, Doug says, "Maggie's would be nowhere."[23]

Worker–owned production model

Since 1999, Maggie's has been absolutely committed to partnering with worker-owned co-operatives. As noted earlier, Maggie's first co-op partner, The Fair Trade Zone co-operative in Nueva Vida, Nicaragua, is the world's first and only 100% worker-owned free trade zone. Building on the success of its partnership with the FTZ co-operative, Maggie's has partnered with, or supported, the development of additional co-operatives in Nicaragua, Costa Rica, and North Carolina.

- In Nicaragua, Maggie's is supporting the development of a spinning co-operative next door to FTZ, which will spin all of the cotton yarn for its sister co-operative

- In Costa Rica, Maggie's has partnered with a 100% worker-owned co-operative

- In rural North Carolina, Maggie's is developing another 100% worker-owned co-operative

Bená believes there is a great opportunity for expanding the worker-owned co-operative model in the U.S., as a way to create empowering economic opportunities for low-income communities.

---

22 "Clothes for a Change — Leaders of the Apparel Industry," OCA (Organic Consumers Association); www.organicconsumers.org/clothes/leaders.cfm, accessed January 29, 2009.
23 Personal communication with D. Wilson, Ypsilanti, MI, February 20, 2008.

Natural food distribution channel

Doug says that selling Maggie's apparel products through food distributors is like having "an oil product in a water distributor."[24] This is because Maggie's fights "tooth and nail" to stay in these channels. On one hand, with no other organic apparel companies selling products in these stores, Maggie's has an incredible advantage. However, when distributors and retailers balk at selling Maggie's products through traditional food channels, the sales team must work hard to sell them on their products' advantages, i.e., no shelf-life, price competitiveness, quality, and, most importantly, consumer demand.

Challenges for the future

Market risks

Increasing competition

As the oldest organic apparel company in the U.S., Maggie's had first-mover advantage in the industry. It has maintained its competitive advantage, in part, through its position as the sole organic apparel company working with the country's three largest natural food distributors. But, in recent years, increasing consumer demand for organic products has opened the floodgates for a slew of new companies — many of whom enter the field armed with dynamic founders and exciting stories.

Increasing competition on the organic apparel shelves of Whole Foods is a sign of the times, and the challenge for Maggie's will be to keep its brand top-of-mind with the retailers. The long-standing relationships that Maggie's has fostered with its retailers will help the company to some degree, but the introduction of fresh, new products and marketing materials will be important elements as well.

Future of the economy

The significant growth of the organics industry since 2000 is owed, at least in part, to consumers' willingness to pay a premium price for the certified organic label. Doug comments that this may be why Wal-Mart

24   Personal communication with D. Wilson, Ypsilanti, MI, February 20, 2008.

does not tout its own category of organic products, which it introduced a couple of years ago.[25] Wal-Mart built its brand on low cost and the Wal-Mart consumer does not appear to be willing to pay a premium for any product.

The future growth of Maggie's and the U.S. organic products industry as a whole is dependent on the economic health of the country. In a period of economic recession, the size of the population with disposable income will shrink and the willingness to pay a premium for organic products may follow suit.

Organizational risks

Maintaining commitment to fair trade

Increasing costs (e.g., rising fuel costs, wages in developing countries, etc.) and increasing competition from goods made in countries such as China — from which Maggie's refuses to source or produce its materials — will continue to pressure its margins. These factors, combined with a potential economic recession, will make it increasingly difficult for Maggie's to maintain its profitability and its commitment to fair prices to producers.

Quality control

Doug says that, "We deal with quality issues every day."[26] The issue of quality control becomes more complex as Maggie's adds new production partners, and as existing production partners become more independent.

As the company continues to grow, it needs to find ways to mitigate the risks associated with poor quality, while maintaining its commitment to supporting and developing the co-operative model of production. Useful methods for doing this include:

1. Maintaining open lines of communication with the production facilities

2. Keeping producers accountable for their quality mistakes through financial penalties

25 Personal communication with D. Wilson, Ypsilanti, MI, February 20, 2008.
26 Personal communication with D. Wilson, Ypsilanti, MI, January 24, 2008.

If expectations and consequences are clearly understood, this will provide a foundation for handling issues as they arise.

Copycat competitors

Maggie's spends significant resources working with partners to develop new methods of production and new types of packaging. For example, Maggie's spent three months working with a manufacturer to develop a post-consumer recycled hanger, adapted to both baby apparel and accessories. As a result, this manufacturer is becoming *the* source for eco-apparel packaging, and several competitors are scheduled to debut products using adaptations of this post-consumer hanger. So, competitors benefit greatly from the time and resources Maggie's spent in developing this innovative new packaging. This pattern will continue in the future, and, while it is not a problem that is unique to Maggie's, it is a risk associated with being an innovator in the industry.

CASE STUDY
PAX Scientific — learning to run

Introduction

Based in San Rafael, CA, PAX Scientific and its family of companies take inspiration from nature with the intention to return the favor. With a focus on energy-efficient products, PAX is the culmination of founder Jayden Harman's unique vision. Growing since 1997, PAX is now a suite of companies employing similar fluid-handling technology in a variety of markets. See Table 16 for an overview of the company.

With a passionate commitment to work in harmony with the Earth's processes, PAX has reached a potential tipping point of influence and success. An outside investment in 2008 instantly doubled the capital infusion into the business and led PAX into a new era of the organization's history.

PAX evolved slowly and with limited success in its first ten years of existence. Through patience and some stumbles, PAX has learned to move from a "crawl" to a "walk." Eyeing market shifts that favor PAX's position in the clean tech market, the company made a deliberate decision to accelerate the business to a "run." The future success of this hybrid will rely on its ability to manage its environmental mission priorities while growing at a venture capitalist's pace.

TABLE 16 PAX Scientific overview

PAX Scientific in 2008	
Year founded:	1997
Annual revenue:	$5 million
No. of employees:	35
Headquarters:	San Rafael, CA, USA
Environmental focus:	• Clean energy • Clean water • Clean air
Profitability level:	Profitable for several years

Mission

PAX applies nature's core design principles to engineer energy–efficient products that enhance and sustain life on Earth.

Overview and history

Using the Latin word for "peace," PAX Scientific is an engineering research and development company that employs unique, patented design geometries inspired by biomimicry to improve fluid-handling equipment. Biomimicry, whose etymology is *bios*, meaning life, and *mimesis*, meaning imitate, imitates nature's most ingenious processes in order to solve human problems. Janine Benyus, founder of the Biomimicry Institute and noted author, calls it "innovation inspired by nature."[1] Figure 31 illustrates some of PAX's designs.

Jay Harman, a native Australian and serial entrepreneur, along with Francesca Bertone, his business partner, wife, and COO, launched PAX Scientific in 1997.

PAX Scientific embodies Jay's life work and passion in studying nature's vortex. "I love nature, and I hate waste," Jay says. "I'd have to say, in every case I've ever seen, nature is still the supreme designer."[2] Whereas nature's system is passive, the human approach is to attack engineering challenges with force, such as hitting or exploding. Vortices — or spiral

1 www.biomimicryinstitute.org, accessed March 30, 2008.
2 Personal communication with J. Harman, San Rafael, CA, January 31, 2008.

FIGURE 31 PAX biomimicry designs: climate vortices on PAX fan models
and fern structure on PAX mixers models

motions of fluid — are fundamentally passive suction systems and the PAX
designs follow this principle.

PAX technology takes advantage of Jay's discovery, the PAX Streamlining Principle, to leverage efficiencies found in nature. These natural
efficiencies can be used to increase efficiency for industrial equipment
such as fans, mixers, propellers, and turbines. The company develops
and licenses its technology to industry leaders in a variety of markets. As
company literature describes:

> Whether pumping water from a well, air-conditioning a build-
> ing, or moving a vehicle down the road, most of the energy
> generated each year is used to overcome drag. In equipment
> designed for handling fluids (such as liquids or gases), poor
> drag control can result in low output or output that is difficult
> to manage, component wear, harmful cavitation, high energy
> use, and excessive noise.[3]

3 Various company materials received from PAX Scientific between November 2007
and January 2008.

Leader-driven mission

PAX is driven by its mission statement, which reads:

> PAX applies nature's core design principles to engineer energy efficient products that enhance and sustain life on Earth.[4]

As Francesca Bertone notes, "We have our eyes on a very big prize . . . reducing energy use on the planet by 20% [by integrating biomimicry design geometries]."[5]

Without formal engineering or design training, Jay has developed some of the most efficient vortices ever created. His design work forms the basis of the company. His vision of the human relation to, and place within, nature guides the PAX family of companies.

Jay grew up in and around the water on the west coast of Australia. As his spouse and business partner says, he "thinks like water."[6] While working for the Australian Department of Fisheries and Wildlife, he started to take particular notice of swirling shapes of water in the ocean. He also entered local politics with the intent to protect Western Australia's sensitive wildlife areas. He worked for years in opposition to developers only to have much of his effort unraveled later on. He became frustrated and came to the conclusion that the world is run by "bean counters." He decided that he had to find a way to show the world that there is value in driving the change he wanted. And the only way he could do this was by doing something that made a profit!

After traveling the world in a sailboat he designed and built, he began his journey as a serial entrepreneur honing his strength in starting companies. He learned many lessons over the course of starting several companies, which ultimately shaped his vision of a company where the vortex pattern he frequently observed in nature might create valuable products. In general, he started small and did not try to accomplish everything at once.

His first company was an electronics company, ERG Australia, which he built through to an initial public offering (IPO). Next he moved to a boat design business, The Serious Boat Company, which included the Wild-Thing and Goggleboat series. It was in this venture that Jay started testing the vortex pattern he had observed as a naturalist. The boats boasted a fuel efficiency 30% greater than comparable vessels. A third successful venture, CSL UK, was a medical research company.

4 Email correspondence with company representatives throughout January 2008.
5 Personal communication with F. Bertone, San Rafael, CA, January 31, 2008.
6 *Ibid.*

Drawing on his previous business ventures, Jay leads PAX to "show manufacturing industries that more efficient equipment is profitable for both shareholders and the planet."[7]

Business strategy and model

Figure 32 depicts PAX's strategy at inception in 1997 and in 2008. PAX has pursued a consistent strategy in designing products for established markets (such as fans and mixers). Its approach to these established markets lies between a same-game strategy and a new-game strategy.

FIGURE 32 PAX's strategic positioning

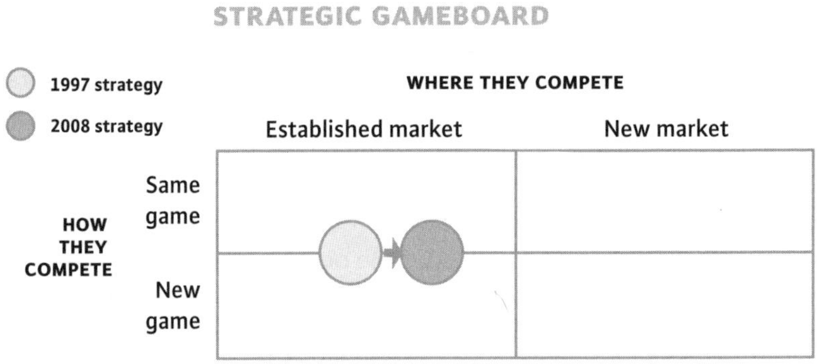

On the one hand, PAX employs a same-game strategy pursuing a similar sales channel as the incumbent technologies. On the other hand, PAX relies on its unique advantage in design geometries to position itself as game-changing. Overall, PAX aims to capitalize on its unique, patented product design to make sweeping changes in any number of industrial applications.

PAX's market development has been modest since its inception. With a culture still more closely resembling an R&D firm than a marketing firm, PAX has struggled to meet its lofty goals.

PAX's market penetration development reflects the evolution from a crawl (concept refinement and product development from 1997 to 2004),

---

7 Personal communication with J. Harman, San Rafael, CA, January 31, 2008.

to a walk (testing a number of market applications from 2004 to 2007), to a run (the launch of PAX Streamline in 2008).

PAX Scientific is composed of a number of companies:

1. Parent company PAX Scientific

2. Subsidiaries PAX Water Technologies and PAX Mixer

Another set of licensee companies, collectively called PaxFan or sometimes the Pax Group, includes PaxIT, PaxFan, and PaxAuto. The PaxFan companies are separately owned and operated companies which have master licenses to commercialize PAX's air handling technologies.

PAX Scientific

Jay was familiar with patent law from his past businesses, and, in 1995, Francesca joined him in Australia where they began patenting his PAX-related designs. They returned to the U.S. in 1997 to establish PAX Scientific with the intention of spending 12–18 months trying to generate interest in its propeller design.

PAX had always intended to focus on the R&D and to avoid manufacturing. After identifying the 22 *Fortune* 100 companies most likely to be interested in its more efficient designs, Jay and Francesca sent each company a one-page letter and received 17 responses of interest. These included responses from such companies as General Dynamics and GE. They began to meet with the companies to explain and demonstrate the design, and expected to make money by licensing it.

Jay and Francesca would attempt to work with executives, but found that most of the companies relied entirely on their suppliers for product development. They then tried to work with the internal R&D teams at these corporations, but found that few companies had "real" R&D anymore — most of the R&D at big manufacturing firms in mature industries is focused on packaging and process, not product development. While companies had plenty of engineers, major product development, for many, was secondary to the more pressing goal of shaving pennies off of each product. PAX ran into further difficulties when companies wanted to test working prototypes, PAX was still in concept phase and unprepared to develop prototypes.

During these early forays, Jay and Francesca concluded that "inertia [was] our greatest obstacle."[8] They spent another year making proto-

---

8 Personal communication with F. Bertone, San Rafael, CA, January 31, 2008.

types, and while the response to the models was nearly always positive, the feedback was that the companies didn't know how to work with PAX. PAX had tried to enter the market at the wrong end of the value chain.

PaxFan, PaxIT, and PaxAuto

By 2001, after several years of refining the product through self-financing, PAX Scientific still had not found a way into the market. The world-changing events of September 11, 2001 provided Jay and Francesca with the impetus to take the company to the next level and, in 2002, they raised capital to expand their business. At that point, they began to prioritize over 500 potential areas of application. The funding enabled the development of a number of prototypes of mixers, fans, and propellers.

An analysis of technology readiness and ease of market entry led the team to focus on air-handling as its first significant commercial push. Jay and Francesca met fellow Bay Area eco-entrepreneur Paul Hawken (of Smith & Hawken garden stores and co-author of *Natural Capitalism*[9]), who encouraged them to start with computer fans since they are easy and inexpensive to test. Further, the potential impact of more efficient computer fans is significant. For example, in a server, there are two to four fans and using a PAX fan can save $1.25/year in electricity cost. A server farm with 100,000 servers using PAX fans could save $500,000/year.

PAX Scientific partnered with Paul Hawken, and he launched the three master licensees — PaxFan, PaxIT, and PaxAuto — each majority-owned and -operated by Paul, with outside funding from Paul's network. Paul and PAX Scientific agreed to a revenue sharing model share in return for the licensed patents. PAX Scientific chose not to have equity or management control in any of the three companies. The intention was to start something small to test the market and allow everyone an easy exit if it did not pan out.

With its prototype computer fans, PaxFan approached computer makers who suggested it talked to the makers of motors. PaxFan subsequently developed relationships with two motor manufacturing companies — AO Smith and Delphi — via license fee agreements. However, PaxFan learned that this approach had flaws. AO Smith did not have a strong strategy or incentive to sell fans, since fans are only a small part of its overall product line; therefore, the distribution of PAX fans via AO Smith has been limited.

9   www.natcap.org

Due to an internal financial restructuring, Delphi has moved slowly for some time but is not increasing its advancement of its sublicensed PAX fan products. Instead, Delphi recently purchased a computer fan manufacturer in Asia to build PAX computer fans.

PAX discovered a couple of surprising findings from the fan commercialization process. First, no one was interested in buying energy efficiency and the story of biomimicry. While the story may have been compelling to executive staff, it didn't matter to the engineering staff. In addition, even if the end-customer might have cared, their market entry point was through distribution and manufacturers. The licensing model, while appropriate given the ecosystem of the fan industry, was frustrating, so, with the next business expansion, PAX decided to take a very different approach.

PAX Water Technologies

In 2006, PAX Water Technologies was established to serve the water and wastewater industries. The stumbles in misjudging the fan industry led to a change in approach to bring in industry experts before entering a new market. For example, to get into the water market, PAX worked for a year studying the best entry point and found potable water mixing as the most viable. Further, it learned to refine the marketing approach; it sells the potable water mixers not for energy efficiency, but for enhanced water quality. Specifically, the water mixers lead to fully mixed water, rather than stagnant stratified tanks that can promote bacterial growth.

The effectiveness of the engineering design results in notable environmental outcomes. The water mixer reduces energy use by 85% and reduces chemical disinfectant use (chemicals used to maintain water quality) by 80%. By way of comparison, a human heart uses approximately 1½ watts of energy to circulate blood throughout the body (approximately one gallon). The PAX water mixer can mix a five million gallon tank with 180 watts of power.

As with PAX Scientific, PAX Water received initial funding from high-net-worth investors and is now selling its product to customers.

PAX Mixer

PAX Mixer is commercializing rotary and static (in-line) mixer technology for the industrial market. These clients include petroleum, pharmaceutical, and beverage industries, which use mixing for product blending, fermentation, suspension, catalysis, crystallization, and two- and three-phase mixing.

Launched in 2007 to address the industrial mixing market, the commercialization approach for PAX Mixer had not been finalized at the time of the case study. The company was evaluating whether to sell directly to the end-user or to license the technologies to various manufacturers.

In October 2007, PAX Scientific was awarded a three-year, $1.9 million Advanced Technology grant from the U.S. Department of Commerce to support development of a new class of industrial mixing technology. PAX Mixer will play a pivotal role in this research for the parent company.

PAX Streamline

PAX Streamline represents the PAX jump into a running mode. Bolstered by significant capital infusion from Khosla Ventures, PAX Streamline was established in late 2007 and spun out from PAX Scientific in early 2008.

PAX Streamline will require R&D to go to market and it will target three to four markets. The company planned to initially target defined markets with established competitors, such as Whirlpool and Carrier. Early targets include:

- Air conditioning

- Turbines (tidal and winglets for wind turbines)

- Aerospace (plane winglets)

- Marine propulsion (propellers)

Within the first 36 months of the investment, the goal was to prove that PAX Streamline could generate a portfolio of applications to draw customers. Future expansion possibilities include a joint venture with a major manufacturing firm or designing software with embedded algorithms.

Finance

Ownership structure — close control

Maintaining control is very important and reflects Jay's previous entrepreneurial experiences. Jay, Francesca, and Laura Bertone, CFO, are the board of directors but Jay and Francesca are majority owners of the subsidiary companies. As such, they directly or indirectly control and manage most of the entire family of PAX companies.

From 1997 to 2007, PAX Scientific and the suite of subsidiaries (not including PAX Streamline) have raised nearly $15 million in capital from close funding sources in relatively modest increments (i.e., primarily from high-net-worth individuals in the founders' network) and government grants. These funding sources were always closely aligned with, and accommodating to, PAX's sustainability mission.

In 2007, a conversation between Francesca and Jay led to the realization that, at the pace they were progressing, they were decades away from realizing their goals. At the same time, it became clear the world (and specifically the U.S.) was recognizing the linked imperatives of solving climate change and reducing energy demand. While PAX had been working slowly and steadily toward the goal, they decided that it was time to ramp up to a run. In January 2008, PAX Streamline closed a $13 million Series A venture financing round led by Khosla Ventures.

PAX had previously turned away venture capital because Jay was concerned about becoming subject to other company's investment goals. One of the best known and respected venture capitalists in the world, Vinod Khosla started a $300 million fund directed toward environmental technologies in 2005. This new fund reflected his personal mission and he pledged all profits toward charity.

Francesca suggested that, within the trident of management choice (see Fig. 33), management can control only two of the three legs. Until the Khosla investment, PAX had chosen a high degree of business impact and strategic control while largely letting return on investment grow organically.

FIGURE 33 Trident of management choice

However, with the decision to accept venture financing for PAX Streamline, there is a distinct focus on the investment return. PAX chose to move
forward with Khosla Ventures because it believed the investment would
generate the business impact it desired. Further, in conversation with
Vinod, Jay and Francesca became convinced that he was not a typical
venture capitalist and that his passive investment approach fitted their
ability to retain a degree of strategic control.

As part of the deal structure, the founders may use organizational con-
trols to keep PAX Streamline on track toward its mission. Specifically, Jay
and Francesca remain the largest shareholders, while Jay is the chairman
of the board and cannot be removed.

Organization

Despite being made up of a number of separate legal entities, all the PAX
companies share the same vision as PAX Scientific, though they execute
that vision in different ways according to their diverse target industries.
The spin-off of PAX Streamline transferred a significant portion of the
patent portfolio and the majority of the PAX Scientific employees to that
entity. Figure 34 shows the organizational structure.

Until the founding of PAX Streamline, PAX Scientific housed all R&D, while
the applications (manufacturing and sales) were executed via subsidiaries. The decision to pursue this model, rather than to develop divisions
within one entity, was driven by two factors. First, there are practical legal
protections of dividing assets and liability protection in separate entities.
Second, the founders hoped that such a structure allowed them to avoid
putting all eggs in one basket. If the technology failed in one application
area, any damage to the overall company — whether financial or reputa-
tion — would be mitigated.

Setting up the recently established PAX Streamline structure, which
will commercialize a number of new areas simultaneously via divisions or
subsidiaries, was a carefully calculated decision. Setting up the previous
subsidiaries and licensees was more organic and part of "simply trying to
run the business as each R&D application area matured."[10]

10 Personal communication with F. Bertone, San Rafael, CA, January 31, 2008.

FIGURE 34 PAX family of businesses

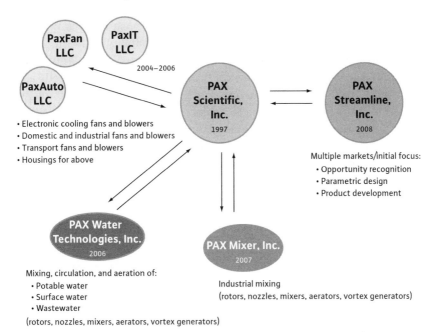

With the expansion into PAX Streamline, Francesca, Laura, and Jay became "much more self-aware" of goals and potential stumbling blocks. Moreover, Francesca noted that "PAX is now at a point in its maturity that they are making decisions with bigger implications" for more employees and are executing grander visions.[11] The result is a completely separate entity with deliberate board control.

Culture and sustainability

Culturally, while the PAX family of businesses operates within defined functional areas, in practice it is a notably flat structure. This is so much the case that, as Laura says, "PAX Scientific has a family atmosphere," which extends beyond the husband–wife–sister executive management team."[12] What is also notable, especially as a research- and engineering-focused company, is that the company has a nearly 50/50 male–female ratio.

11 *Ibid.*
12 Personal communication with L. Bertone, San Rafael, CA, January 31, 2008.

Throughout the organization, they are passionate about sustainability. This passion is one area that exemplifies the engagement of employees at all levels of the company. Staff frequently propose internal changes and internal champions — such as for the sustainability platform, which establishes the principles to reduce the manufacturing environmental footprint. However, goals are always balanced with company needs and finances. Actions are made when they are practical in terms of the time, energy, and the monetary costs to implement.

Each separate business may also have its own approach to sustainability. Figure 35 illustrates the approach of the PAX Water Technologies business unit sustainability.

FIGURE 35 Sustainability at PAX Water

Source: PAX Scientific company materials

PAX Water Technologies sustainability

Our mission is to design and manufacture efficient water mixers that produce minimal impact on the environment.

We assess every step of product development using the following criteria:

1. Does the product achieve the optimum productivity from the minimum amount of **energy** or fuel?
2. Does the product's design optimize the **space** allowed, using the least materials and leaving the smallest possible footprint?
3. Is the product manufactured using non-polluting, efficient, replicable **processes** that place the minimum of strain on workers and ecosystems?
4. Do we address the **environmental** impact of this product at every stage of its design and life cycle — including the end?
5. Is the manufacture and operation of this product safe and non-toxic to the **people** who will be producing and using it?
6. Did we choose **materials** that can be obtained with the least damage to the planet, and can be reused or recycled with likewise minimal damage?
7. Have we identified ways to minimize the **packaging** and **transportation** costs associated with the design, manufacture, sales, and installation of this product?
8. Do we and our vendors abide by all labor and environmental **laws** in the production and implementation of this product?

Processes and metrics

PAX tracks its environmental performance both internally and for downstream product impacts.

Internally, PAX is aware of its resource use, recycling, and product design. For example, staff are well aware of the utensils used, and even proposed moving toward bio-based products to replace any plastic ware used. However, as a small organization with self-selecting employees with a personal environmental awareness, the internal environmental impact pales in comparison to the downstream products. As Paul Hawken advised them, "focus on the big picture — don't worry about whether you only use plastic forks, you're doing something important."[13]

The most obvious downstream impact of PAX products is the reduction of energy sparked by replacing conventionally designed products. PAX is aware of the overall performance of its products and some anecdotal results, but does not keep an aggregated tally. For example, PAX is well aware that its fans are 30% more energy-efficient than those they replace, but lacks a calculation for total energy saved by all PAX fans installed. Where relevant, PAX also notes other environmental performance measures, such as chemicals, water, or wastewater reduced for particular applications.

Innovation

PAX is a leader in biomimicry design for fluid propulsion. The company holds numerous U.S. and international patents to protect its innovative technologies. PAX deploys these innovative designs in a number of market applications. It is both this innovative approach to product design and its application that enables this hybrid organization to meet its mission goals.

Challenges for the future

At of 2008, PAX was on the brink of a major organizational shift with the launch of PAX Streamline. While the existing organizations are deliberately buffered from the stand-alone PAX Streamline, in practical terms the new entity is designed to dominate the family of companies. With the infusion of capital, transfer of intellectual property, and new external pressures to

---

13 Personal communication with F. Bertone, San Rafael, CA, January 31, 2008.

meet milestones, significant resources will shift toward PAX Streamline. Such a change will raise several challenges in the future.

Learning to run

Since its inception in 1997, PAX has developed a number of successful applications, albeit in a measured pace and with several hiccups along the way. The margin and likelihood for future error should be reduced with institutional investors providing resources and pressure to perform. The pace of development will likely accelerate and the organization will be challenged to conform to new expectations.

Maintaining sufficient "impact" and "control'

PAX knows of the shift of management attention toward return on investment (ROI) in the management triad (see Fig. 33) due to the venture capital investment. The PAX mission suggests a clear focus on impact, while leadership personality and organizational design measures point toward a desire for control. The distinct change toward financial performance will necessarily change attention on the other two aspects. While in the short term an appropriate balance may be easily achieved, the venture capitalists' need for an investment exit could represent a significant point of friction. Further, although success will undoubtedly make the balance easier, should PAX fail to meet milestones or other expectations, ROI focus could lead to faltering impact and/or control.

On the other hand, PAX may have found an ability to meet its sustainability mission in conjunction with other demands. Since PAX products result in downstream energy conservation impacts far greater than those they might conserve through internal activities, PAX may meet the business impact goals without any specific attention. Thus, with a focus on the investment return and attention diverted toward strategic control, this clean tech company may master the triad.

Culture change

The PAX family of companies faces an imminent cultural challenge. As the company plans to grow significantly and rapidly, it is aware that consistent culture is more difficult to maintain. The PAX family of businesses will expand to other buildings and the staff will be in multiple places. The whole group of PAX companies currently includes 35 employees and it is already posting jobs for an additional seven positions. Traditionally, PAX has tried not to hire to narrow formulas, and hope to attract self-selecting people who believe in the mission and the PAX approach. The challenge will be in keeping a deeply rooted culture as they grow beyond the "family feel."

10
Business lessons for hybrid organizations

Using the key survey trends emerging from the hybrid sector, we aimed to ground these trends in the context of organizational innovations from the five case studies. These innovations provide lessons for practitioners and researchers of hybrid organizations alike. In particular, the information gleaned from the case studies revealed five common practices that help hybrid organizations reach both their financial and environmental objectives:

- Implementing the mission in action

- Uncommonly close, personal relationships

- Patience

- Limits to growth rate

- Market premium products; rarely compete on price

Lesson I. Implementing the mission in action

Many companies have inspiring mission statements with a goal related to delivering a common good. However, daily decisions may not necessarily reflect that mission. Hybrid organizations distinguish themselves in that their explicit environmental mission is embedded in the business model and is central to every major business decision.

Through the interviews with best-in-class companies, we identified a common theme of creative practices or engrained learning which continually reinforce the mission. Each interviewee clearly identified a strict adherence to mission and talked about why or how their organization's culture is infused with action that aligns with the mission.

- **Eden Foods** demonstrates the mission in action by maintaining a consistent mission since its inception four decades ago. Using oral traditions to communicate how the company began, its key successes and failures, and the personalities behind the business is a key driver for Eden Foods; the story of Eden Foods is so integral that it forms the basis of all product packaging

- Similarly, **Guayakí** literally passes around its mission at company meetings. Passing around a gourd with mate and encouraging employees to share personal as well as professional issues connects the tradition of mate to each other and reinforces the mission

- At SUN OVENS, Paul Munsen, CEO, learned the hard way that business decisions must fit the mission. While short-term opportunities can help build cash flow to offset financial challenges, such opportunities must clearly fit within an overall business strategy such that, when the opportunities disappear, carryover benefits continue to build the organization

- At **Maggie's Organics**, even though there is an environmental mission behind the work, Doug Wilson, VP of Sales, says it's not easy to get all the staff to buy into that mission all the time. "We care about doing the right thing, and we want the people we work with to care about doing the right thing too," says Doug.[1] Bená Burda, founder and President, and Doug work hard to create a team-like atmosphere both within their headquarters as well as with their producers and their customers. This requires constant communication about how and why the business is run

---

1   Personal communication with D. Wilson, Ypsilanti, MI, January 24, 2008.

Lesson II. Uncommonly close, personal relationships

Hybrid organizations operate in clear contrast to the cliché, "it isn't personal, it's business." Much of the success of these organizations in meeting their missions stems from the uncommonly close relationships they foster with suppliers, producers, and customers. Throughout the chain of delivering products to the marketplace, hybrid organizations' senior management often have personal connections to supply chain partners, customers, and stakeholders. While this may be partially a function of small company size, case study insight suggests this is a deliberate business decision.

- An integral part of the **Maggie's Organics** business model involves developing strong relationships with the people making the products and the people buying the products. What differentiates Maggie's from traditional supply chains is the ability to use packaging and marketing materials to connect the end-consumer with the "story" behind the product and the producers. This connection, combined with a top-quality product, results in satisfied consumers who understand that their purchases contribute to a business ecosystem that provides benefit for everyone in it

- Similarly, the most innovative aspect of **Eden Foods**, according to Michael Potter, CEO, is the personal relationships the company maintains with all the supplier farmers and their families. For example, the idea to can organic beans started from an excess of products from the farmers, leading Eden to look into a way of preserving the beans and ensuring that the farmers continue to sell the beans for an organic price premium. This close relationship with growers has proven to be a competitive advantage for them

- For SUN OVENS, reaching the highly sought-after, but often remote, customer is a huge challenge requiring resources and creativity that exceed what is typically required by traditional companies. The company's use of hands-on educational workshops goes far beyond traditional product demonstration, consumer research, and financing support

- At PAX **Scientific**, shareholders can feel like family. Since patient shareholders believe in environmental impact goals, they are not necessarily focused on the speed and magnitude of financial returns in the same way that traditional investors might be

Lesson III. Patience

Many hybrid organizations pursue generational or multi-generational changes. Seventh Generation demonstrates this in its company's name, derived from the Law of the Iroquois that decrees, "In our every deliberation, we must consider the impact of our decisions on the next seven generations."[2] With such ambitious missions, hybrid organizations, in contrast to traditional businesses, often have longer time-frames to reach maturity, which requires greater patience for all stakeholders.

- At **Guayakí**, the team has found that it can take generations to change people's habits. Accordingly, bringing mate into a market that is dominated by coffee has been a challenge. However, the company has learned that persistence and patience are critical to its marketing efforts and that it takes a long time to build a long-term dependable supply of mate. As Chris Mann, CEO, says: "it can take generations to change a habit and perhaps longer to change economics."[3]

- For **PAX Scientific**, it has been a long progression from crawling, to walking, to running. It took nearly ten years for the company to achieve noteworthy market penetration, and only recently has it matured from crawling to walking. As detailed in the case study, PAX is just now getting ready to run

Lesson IV. Limits to growth rate

As hybrid organizations attempt to scale their business, they are likely to find themselves facing a dilemma pitting their mission against financial value. Not to be confused with a limit to overall growth, often at times there are distinct beliefs in a limit to the **rate** of growth. One of Clif Bar's Five Aspirations, for example, is to "*grow slower*, grow better and stick around longer" (our emphasis).

The case studies in this book help illustrate the tension and decision-making process that hybrids face when choosing how fast to reach both mission and market.

---

2 Seventh Generation website: www.seventhgeneration.com/about, accessed January 15, 2008.
3 Personal communication with C. Mann, Sebastopol, CA, January 31, 2008.

- **Guayakí** believes there is a limit to how fast an organization can grow if it wants to stay true to its mission. While the Guayakí team believes that market demand exists to grow the company from $10 million in sales to $30 million in sales in the span of a couple of years, Chris Mann believes it would be impossible to do so while still remaining true to the Atlantic Rainforest:

  > We have to make sure our product is sustainable and it takes more time. Other companies, who do not take [mission-driven] sourcing into consideration, would be able to scale up much faster.[4]

- For SUN OVENS, one might argue that chasing after a fleeting Y2K market forced the company to develop too fast and, as of 2008, the company still struggled with the debt obligation of those early-stage decisions. The company has subsequently learned to balance its environmental and social mission with financial goals in every corporate decision — whether it be a financial decision to sell off shares of the company to outside investors, or an operational decision to allocate scarce resources to developing markets instead of developed markets. SUN OVENS has realized that, to be a long-lasting business, a hybrid organization has to carefully manage growth in light of its triple-bottom-line approach

Lesson V. Market premium products; rarely compete on price

Our analysis of hybrid organizations reveals a distinct trend of premium product offerings and rare price advantage. The case studies reinforce this notion, as several of the companies are the distinct quality market leaders in their industry. This suggests that, while companies may tweak their product for larger mass appeal, they often pursue new game strategies that incorporate novel market segments or product categories rather than competing directly in an established market or product.

- At **Eden Foods**, the mission is to provide the highest-quality, organic, wholesome foods for its customers. While this may seem like a traditional mission statement, no one in the company seems willing to compromise on product quality. In the words of

---

4 Personal communication with C. Mann, Sebastopol, CA, January 31, 2008.

Sue Becker, Director and VP of Marketing, "We do it the hard way. We do it the right way and that gives me peace of mind to sleep at night."[5] While this uncompromising attitude is essential to the mission, it often cuts into the profit margin of the company. For example, Eden Foods, on average, pays a higher price for its raw materials

- **Maggie's Organics** achieved a competitive advantage by creating an entirely novel distribution channel for its organic clothing — natural foods retailers. Because Maggie's was one of the first companies to sell organic apparel in the U.S., no distribution channel for these types of products existed. However, Bená Burda realized from the outset that the organic food consumer was much more likely to buy Maggie's products than the traditional apparel consumer, and she was subsequently able to make the right connections to create a new distribution channel

- **Guayakí** consumers are willing to pay more for its products. Part of that premium is the result of Guayakí's sustainability mission and part results from its superior product. While the combination of premium product and sustainability inherently limits Guayakí's market share, traditional for-profit businesses are unlikely to feel this same combination of constraints

It should be noted that no single one of the above practices sets apart a hybrid organization from a traditional for-profit or nonprofit organization. Instead, it is the combination of these innovative practices that allows hybrids to meet their mission- and market-centric goals in an effective manner. Hybrid organizations utilize an integrated system of non-traditional business activities that allow them to bridge the gap between mission and finance. It is this integration of activities that truly sets hybrid organizations apart.

---

5 Personal communication with S. Becker, Clinton, MI, January 11, 2008.

11
Reflecting back, looking forward

This book has aimed to explore the challenges, solutions, trends, and lessons learned from innovative, sustainability-driven, hybrid organizations that use a variety of organizational elements to meet their mission. We hypothesized that hybrid organizations can be an effective structure to create positive contributions to humanity's most pressing challenges. Drawing on the results of a literature review, we identified a research gap which suggested that privately owned hybrid organizations with a focus on environmental sustainability would be of particular interest to test this notion.

Using a broad-based survey and in-depth case studies, the study revealed a number of recent trends in the hybrid organizations sector. By analyzing the survey data from 47 innovative hybrid organizations, we gained insight into the elements that help characterize hybrid organizations.

The best-in-class case studies imparted valuable lessons and guidance as to how hybrid organizations are succeeding in meeting their environmental mission and financial goals. Five recurring business practices, as reiterated in Table 17, suggest that hybrid organizations are indeed effective vehicles to promoting environmental sustainability. However, some limits and constraints to their scale and impact exist, and opportunities outside the scope of this project suggest future areas for investigation.

TABLE 17 Lessons for hybrid organizations

Hybrid practice	Illustrative cases
Implementing the mission in action	• Eden Foods • Guayakí • Maggie's Organics • SUN OVENS International
Uncommonly close, personal relationships	• Eden Foods • Maggie's Organics • PAX Scientific • SUN OVENS International
Patience	• Guayakí • PAX Scientific
Limits to growth rate	• Guayakí • SUN OVENS International
Market premium products; rarely compete on price	• Eden Foods • Guayakí • Maggie's Organics

Hybrid organization: definition revisited

As any business leader knows, it is not just one element of an organization that allows a company to create a sustainable competitive edge over its competitors, but the entire system of strategic and operational elements. Similarly for hybrids, it is not just one or two of these innovations that define hybrid organizations; but rather the integration of all such elements creates an organizational form distinct from traditional models. By combining innovative business practices that allow the organization to meet mission- and market-centric goals, a hybrid organization can alleviate the world's most pressing issues.

Hybrid organization: effectiveness revisited

Central to this study was the question, "Are hybrids successful at achieving environmentally sustainability?" The insights described in this book
reveal that some hybrid organizations are quite successful in achieving
both their environmental sustainability and financial profitability goals.
Others are much more successful at achieving one or the other. Still others have yet to achieve success in either. Regardless, the survey results
and case studies provide evidence of profitable companies with embedded business practices helping them meet their environmental mission.
These companies are effectively bridging the gap between for-profit and
nonprofit aims within one organization. Such companies are restoring
and/or promoting healthy farm and forest land, contributing to healthy
ecosystems, and moving toward renewable resource use as they shift
from non-renewable resources.

However, analysis of the sample set of hybrid organizations in this
study also suggests that, as relatively young companies with limited
track records, their environmental sustainability activities have limited
scale and impact. With potential limits to growth, questions remain about
whether hybrid organizations can effectively scale up to meet global challenges. On one hand, it may be that some environmental sustainability
goals — such as clean air, clean water, and clean energy — are likely to
have economies of scale that make faster growth and mission impact
more easily achievable. On the other, sustainable agriculture practices
implicitly or explicitly shun economies of scale. Particularly in the case
of place-based business models, scalability may be a limiting factor for
hybrids to consider.

At this point, the research suggests that hybrid organizations represent
a small subset of privately owned companies which, while they have had
some success in reaching their targeted goals, are cumulatively overshad-
owed by larger institutions. However, lessons from hybrids, such as methods for embedding the mission in the organization, may be applicable
for larger entities. While broad efforts by multinational corporations or
international NGOs may appear to have widespread results, hybrid organizations can also be very efficient and self-sufficient in meeting global
environmental sustainability challenges, even while reaching currently
hard-to-reach markets.

Overall, this research into environmental sustainability-driven hybrid
organizations suggests that this organizational form is a viable model and

effectively meets a range of global environmental challenges. While there may be limits in the speed and scale in which these hybrid organizations can thrive, they may also ultimately be more effective and more self-sustaining than traditional for-profit or nonprofit organizations.

References

Abrahamsson, A. (2007) *Sustainopreneurship: Business with a Cause* (Växjö, Sweden: Växjö University, School of Management and Economics).

Alexander, J. (2000) "Adaptive Strategies of Nonprofit Human Service Organizations in an Era of Devolution and New Public Management," *Nonprofit Management and Leadership* 10.3: 287-303.

Alkhafaji, A.F. (1989) *A Stakeholder Approach to Corporate Governance: Managing in a Dynamic Environment* (New York: Quorum Books).

Alter, K. (2004). *Social Enterprise Typology* (Seattle, WA: Virtue Ventures LLC).

Alvord, S.H., L.D. Brown, and C.W. Letts (2004) "Social Entrepreneurship and Societal Transformation: An Exploratory Study," *Journal of Applied Behavioral Science* 40.3: 260-82.

Anderson, J.C., and A.W. Frankle (1980) "Voluntary Social Reporting: An Iso-Beta Portfolio Analysis." *The Accounting Review* 55.3: 467-79.

Arts, B. (2002) "Green Alliances" of Business and NGOs. New Styles of Self-regulation or "Dead-end Roads?" *Corporate Social Responsibility and Environmental Management* 9.1: 26-36.

Aupperle, K.E., A.B. Carroll, and J.D. Hatfield (1985) "An Empirical Examination of the Relationship between Corporate Social Responsibility and Profitability," *Academy of Management Journal* 28.2: 446-63.

Austin, J.E. (2000) *The Collaboration Challenge: How Nonprofits and Businesses Succeed through Strategic Alliances* (San Francisco: Jossey-Bass).

——, R. Gutiérrez, E. Ogliastri, and E. Reficco (2007) "Capitalizing on Convergence," *Stanford Social Innovation Review* 5.1: 24-31.

Beheiry, S.M.A., W.K. Chong, M. Asce, and C.T. Haas (2006) "Examining the Business Impact of Owner Commitment to Sustainability," *Journal of Construction Engineering and Management* 132: 384-92.

Bendell, J. (ed.) (2000) *Terms for Endearment: Business, NGOs and Sustainable Development* (Sheffield, UK: Greenleaf Publishing).

Bennett, S.J. (1991) *Ecopreneuring: The Complete Guide to Small Business Opportunities from the Environmental Revolution* (New York: John Wiley).

Berle, G. (1991) *The Green Entrepreneur: Business Opportunities That Can Save the Earth Make you Money* (Blue Ridge Summit, PA: TAB Books Inc.).

Billitteri, T.J. (2007) *Mixing Mission and Business: Does Social Enterprise Need a New Legal Approach?* (Washington, DC: Nonprofit Sector Research Fund, The Aspen Institute).

Birkin, F., T. Polesie, and L. Lewis (2007) "A New Business Model for Sustainable Development: An Exploratory Study Using the Theory of Constraints in Nordic Organizations," *Business Strategy and the Environment*, published online 8 May 2007.

——, A. Cashman, S.C.L. Koh, and Z. Liu (2009) "New Sustainable Business Models in China," *Business Strategy and the Environment* 18.1, 64-77; published online 13 February 2007.

Blue, R.J. (1990) *Ecopreneuring: Managing for Results* (London: Scott Foresman).

Boschee, J. (2001) *The Social Enterprise Sourcebook: Profiles of Social Purpose Businesses Operated by Nonprofit Organizations* (Minneapolis, MN: Northland Institute).

—— and J. McClurg (2003) *Toward a Better Understanding of Social Entrepreneurship: Some Important Distinctions* (Columbus, OH: Social Enterprise Alliance; www.sealliance.org/better_understanding.pdf, accessed January 29, 2009).

Bowman, E.H., and M. Haire (1975) "A Strategic Posture toward Corporate Social Responsibility," *California Management Review* 18.2: 49-58.

Brandsen, T., W. van de Donk, and K. Putters (2005) "Griffins or Chameleons? Hybridity as a Permanent and Inevitable Characteristic of the Third Sector," *International Journal of Public Administration* 28.9: 749-65.

Brown, C.S., and NetLibrary Inc. (2005) *The Sustainable Enterprise Profiting from Best Practice* (London/Sterling, VA: Kogan Page).

Burke, L., and J.M. Logsdon (1996) "How Corporate Social Responsibility Pays Off," *Long Range Planning* 29.4: 495-502.

Carroll, A.B. (1999) "Corporate Social Responsibility: Evolution of a Definitional Construct," *Business & Society* 38.3: 268-95.

Casselman, B. (2007) "Giving Back: Why 'Social Enterprise' Rarely Works," *Wall Street Journal*, June 1, 2007.

Cohen, B., and M. Winn (2005) "Market Imperfections, Opportunity and Sustainable Entrepreneurship," *Journal of Business Venturing* 22.1: 29-49.

Cooney, K. (2006) "The Institutional and Technical Structuring of Nonprofit Ventures: Case Study of a U.S. Hybrid Organization Caught between Two Fields," *Voluntas: International Journal of Voluntary and Nonprofit Organizations* 17.2: 137-55.

Conaty, P. (2001) *Homeopathic Finance: Equitable Capital for Social Enterprises* (London: New Economics Foundation).

Cornell, B., and A.C. Shapiro (1987) "Corporate Stakeholders and Corporate Finance," *Financial Management* 16.1: 5-14.

Crals, E., and L. Vereeck (2004) "Sustainable Entrepreneurship in SMEs: Theory and Practice," paper presented at the *Third Global Conference on Environmental Justice and Global Citizenship*, Copenhagen, February 12–14, 2004.

Dacin, M.T., C. Oliver, and J.P. Roy (2007) "The Legitimacy of Strategic Alliances: An Institutional Perspective," *Strategic Management Journal* 28: 169-87.

Davis, K. (1960) "Can Business Afford to Ignore Social Responsibility?" *California Management Review* 2.3: 70-6.

Davis, L. (1998) *The NGO–Business Hybrid: Is the Private Sector the Answer?* (Washington, DC: Paul H. Nitze School of Advanced International Studies; Baltimore, MD: Johns Hopkins University).

Dees, J.G. (1998a) "The Meaning of Social Entrepreneurship," Stanford Business School, The Center for Social Innovation; www.fuqua.duke.edu/centers/case/documents/dees_SE.pdf, accessed January 29, 2009.

—— (1998b) "Enterprising Nonprofits," *Harvard Business Review* 76.1: 55-67.

——, B.B. Anderson, and J. Wei-Skillern (2004) "Scaling Social Impact," *Stanford Social Innovation Review* 1.4: 24-32.

Déniz-Déniz, M.C., and J.M. García-Falcón (2002) "Determinants of the Multinationals' Social Response: Empirical Application to International Companies Operating in Spain," *Journal of Business Ethics* 38.4: 339-70.

Dentchev, N.A. (2004) "Corporate Social Performance as a Business Strategy," *Journal of Business Ethics* 55.4: 395-410.

Dixon, S.E.A., and A. Clifford (2007) "Ecopreneurship: A New Approach to Managing the Triple Bottom Line," *Journal of Organizational Change Management* 20.3: 326-45.

Draper, L. (2005) "Tapping Overlooked Sources of Support for Nonprofits," *Foundation News & Commentary* 46.1: 27-32.

Drucker, P.F. (2006) *Innovation and Entrepreneurship* (London: HarperCollins).

Eden Foods (2007) *Eden Organic 2007–2008 Catalog* (Clinton, MI: Eden Foods Inc.).

EJF (Environmental Justice Foundation) (2007) "The Deadly Chemicals in Cotton" (London: EJF in collaboration with Pesticide Action Network UK; www.ejfoundation.org/pdf/the_deadly_chemicals_in_cotton.pdf, accessed January 29, 2009).

Emerson, J., and S. Bonini (2003) "Blended Value Map: Executive Summary"; www.blendedvalue.org/publications/index.html#summary, accessed January 29, 2009.

—— and F. Twersky (1996) *New Social Entrepreneurs: The Success, Challenge and Lessons of Non-profit Enterprise Creation* (San Francisco: Homeless Economic Development Fund, Roberts Foundation).

Engen, T. (2005) "Sustainable Business: The Need for New Business Models in a Changing World," address by Travis Engen, President and Chief Executive Officer, Alcan Inc., at the Birkbeck Lecture Series, London, October 27, 2005.

Epstein, M.J., and M. Roy (2003) "Making the Business Case for Sustainability," *Journal of Corporate Citizenship* 9: 79-96.

Etchart, N., and L. Davis (2003) "Unique and Universal: Lessons from the Emerging Field of Social Enterprise in Emerging Market Countries" (Turlock, CA: NESsT; www.nesst.org/documents/NESsTUniqueandUniversalpaperMay2003.pdf, accessed January 29, 2009).

Foster, W., and J. Bradach (2005) "Should Nonprofits Seek Profits?" *Harvard Business Review* 83.2: 92-100.

Freedman, M., and B. Jaggi (1982) "Pollution Disclosures, Pollution Performance and Economic Performance," *Omega* 10.2: 167-76.

Friedman, M. (1962) *Capitalism and Freedom* (Chicago: University of Chicago Press).

Gerlach, A. (2003a) "Innovativität und Sustainability Intrapreneurship," paper presented at *Sustainable Management in Action '03*, University of St Gallen, Switzerland.

—— (2003b) "Sustainable Entrepreneurship and Innovation," paper presented at *Corporate Social Responsibility and Environmental Management 2003,* Leeds, UK, May 30–June 1, 2003.

Hall, D.L. (2005) *Business Opportunities for Nonprofits: A Primer on Social Enterprise Ventures* (Pittsburg, PA: University of Pittsburgh).

Hart, S.L. (2005) *Capitalism at the Crossroads: The Unlimited Business Opportunities in Solving the World's Most Difficult Problems* (Upper Saddle River, NJ: Wharton School Publishing).

Haugh, H. (2005) "A Research Agenda for Social Entrepreneurship," *Social Enterprise Journal* 1.1: 1-12.

Heck, C.I., and E.G. de Mejia (2007) "Yerba Mate Tea (*Ilex paraguariensis*): A Comprehensive Review on Chemistry, Health Implications, and Technological Considerations," *Journal of Food Science* 72.9: 1,966-73.

Heritage, W.H.J., and T.J. Orlebeke (2004) "Legal and Tax Considerations," in C. Massarsky, S. Oster, and S. Beinhacker (eds.), *Generating and Sustaining Nonprofit Earned Income* (San Francisco: Jossey-Bass): 77-95.

Hillman, A.J., and G.D. Keim (2001) "Shareholder Value, Stakeholder Management, and Social Issues: What's the Bottom Line?" *Strategic Management Journal* 22.2: 125-39.

Hockerts, K.N. (2003) *Sustainability Innovations: Ecological and Social Entrepreneurship and the Managing of Antagonistic Assets* (St Gallen, Switzerland: University of St Gallen).

Hoffman, A.J. (2000) *Competitive Environmental Strategy: A Guide to the Changing Business Landscape* (Washington, DC: Island Press).

—— (2006) "The Object of Change" (Managing Organizational Change NRE 501; Ann Arbor, MI: University of Michigan, March 9, 2006).

Hudnut, P., T. Bauer, and N. Lorenz (2006) "Appropriate Organizational Design: A Hybrid Business Model for Technology Transfer to the Developing World"; www.nciia.net/conf_06/papers/pdf/hudnut.pdf, accessed May 7, 2009.

IEA (International Energy Agency) (2006) "Energy for Cooking in Developing Countries," in *World Energy Outlook 2006* (Paris: International Energy Agency; www.worldenergyoutlook.org/2006.asp, accessed January 29, 2009): 419-55.

Johnson, S. (2000) "Literature Review on Social Entrepreneurship," Canadian Centre for Social Entrepreneurship; www.business.ualberta.ca/ccse/publications/default.htm, accessed January 29, 2009.

Keijzers, G. (2002) "The Transition to the Sustainable Enterprise," *Journal of Cleaner Production* 10.4: 349-59.

Kraft, K.L., and J. Hage (1990) "Strategy, Social Responsibility and Implementation," *Journal of Business Ethics* 9.1: 11-19.

Marz, J.W., T.L. Powers, and T. Queisser (2003) "Corporate and Individual Influences on Managers' Social Orientation," *Journal of Business Ethics* 46.1: 1-11.

Massarsky, C.W., and S.L. Beinhacker (2002) *Enterprising Nonprofits: Revenue Generation in the Nonprofit Sector* (Englewood Cliffs, NJ: Yale School of Management and The Goldman Sachs Foundation Partnership on Nonprofit Ventures for The Pew Charitable Trusts).

McGuire, J.B., A. Sundgren, and T. Schneeweis (1988) "Corporate Social Responsibility and Firm Financial Performance," *Academy of Management Journal* 31.4: 854-72.

McWilliams, A., and D. Siegel (2000) "Research Notes and Communications: Corporate Social Responsibility and Financial Performance: Correlation or Misspecification," *Strategic Management Journal* 21: 603-609.

Oliver, H. (2007) "Bená Burda of Maggie's Organics Puts an Organic Spin on Cotton," Organic Consumers Association; www.organicconsumers.org/articles/article_7092.cfm, accessed January 29, 2009.

Organic Exchange (2006) "Organic Cotton Market Report: Executive Summary. Spring 2006"; www.organicexchange.org/Documents/marketreport_2006.pdf, accessed January 29, 2009.

OTA (Organic Trade Association) (2007) "Organic Trade Association's American Organic Standards for Fiber," www.ota.com/AmericanOrganicStandardsforFiber. html, accessed January 29, 2009.

—— (2008) "Organic Trade Association's 2007 Manufacturer Survey, conducted by Packaged Facts: Executive Summary"; www.ota.com/pics/documents/ 2007ExecutiveSummary.pdf, accessed January 29, 2009.

Parrish, B.D. (2005) "A Value-Based Model of Sustainable Enterprise," paper presented at the *Business Strategy and the Environment Conference*, Leeds, UK, June 5–6, 2005.

Pava, M.L., and J. Krausz (1996) "The Association between Corporate Social Responsibility and Financial Performance: The Paradox of Social Cost," *Journal of Business Ethics* 15.3: 321-57.

Peredo, A.M., and M. McLean (2006) "Social Entrepreneurship: A Critical Review of the Concept," *Journal of World Business* 41.1: 56-65.

Posner, E.A., and A. Malani (2006) *The Case for For-profit Charities* (Chicago: University of Chicago Law School).

Posner, B.Z., and W.H. Schmidt (1992) "Values and the American Manager: An Update Updated," *California Management Review* 34.3: 80-94.

Prahalad, C.K. (2005) *The Fortune at the Bottom of the Pyramid: Eradicating Poverty through Profits* (Upper Saddle River, NJ: Wharton School Publishing).

Preston, L.E., and D.P. O'Bannon (1997) "The Corporate Social–Financial Performance Relationship: A Typology and Analysis," *Business & Society* 36.4: 419-29.

Quazi, A.M., and D. O'Brien (2000) "An Empirical Test of a Cross-national Model of Corporate Social Responsibility," *Journal of Business Ethics* 25.1: 33-51.

Rasiel, E.M., and P.N. Friga (2001) *The McKinsey Mind: Understanding and Implementing the Problem-Solving Tools and Management Techniques of the World's Top Strategic Consulting Firm* (New York: McGraw-Hill).

Reed, D.J., and WRI (World Resources Institute) (2001) *Stalking the Elusive Business Case for Corporate Sustainability* (Washington, DC: WRI).

Reis, T.K., and S.J. Clohesy (2001) "Unleashing New Resources and Entrepreneurship for the Common Good: A Philanthropic Renaissance," *New Directions for Philanthropic Fundraising* 2001.32: 109-44.

Robinson, J. (2004) "Squaring the Circle? Some Thoughts on the Idea of Sustainable Development," *Ecological Economics* 48.4: 369-84.

Rojšek, I. (2001) "From Red to Green: Towards the Environmental Management in the Country in Transition," *Journal of Business Ethics* 33.1: 37-50.

Sachs, J.D. (2005) *Investing in Development: A Practical Plan to Achieve the Millennium Development Goals* (London: Earthscan).

Salzmann, O., A. Ionescu-Somers, and U. Steger (2005) "The Business Case for Corporate Sustainability: Literature Review and Research Options," *European Management Journal* 23.1: 27-36.

Schaltegger, S. (2000) "Vom Bionier zum Sustainopreneur," paper presented at *Rio Impuls Management Forum 2000,* Lucerne, Switzerland, November 10, 2000; www. rio.ch/Pages/rmf2000/referate/Schaltegger.pdf, accessed January 29, 2009.

Schaper, M. (2002) "The Essence of Ecopreneurship," *Greener Management International* 38: 26-30.

—— (2005) *Making Ecopreneurs: Developing Sustainable Entrepreneurship* (Aldershot, UK: Ashgate Publishing).

Schumpeter, J.A. (1989) *Essays: On Entrepreneurs, Innovations, Business Cycles, and the Evolution of Capitalism* (Edison, NJ: Transaction Publishers).

Shaw, E., J. Shaw, and M. Wilson (2002) *Unsung Entrepreneurs: Entrepreneurship for Social Gain* (Durham, UK: University of Durham Business School).

Smallbone, D., M. Evans, I. Ekanem, and S. Butters (2001) "Researching Social Enterprise," Final Report to the Small Business Service, Centre for Enterprise and Economic Development Research, Middlesex University, London; www.berr.gov. uk/files/file38361.pdf, accessed January 29, 2009.

Stanwick, P.A., and S.D. Stanwick (1998) "The Relationship between Corporate Social Performance, and Organizational Size, Financial Performance, and Environmental Performance: An Empirical Examination," *Journal of Business Ethics* 17.2: 195-204.

Strom, S. (2007) "Make Money, Save the World," *New York Times,* May 6, 2007.

SustainAbility (2007) "Growing Opportunity: Entrepreneurial Solutions to Insoluble Problems," SustainAbility and the Skoll Foundation; www.sustainability.com/compass/download_file.asp?articleid=250, accessed January 29, 2009.

Swanson, D.L. (1999) "Toward an Integrative Theory of Business and Society: A Research Strategy for Corporate Social Performance," *The Academy of Management Review* 24.3: 506-21.

Taylor, N., R. Hobbs, F. Nilsson, K. O'Halloran, and C. Preisser (2000) "The Rise of the Term Social Entrepreneurship in Print Publications," in *Frontiers of Entrepreneurship Research: Proceedings of the Annual Babson College Entrepreneurship Research Conference*, Babson Park, MA: 466.

Vance, S.C. (1975) "Are Socially Responsible Corporations Good Investment Risks?" *Management Review* 64.8: 19-24.

Waddock, S.A., and S.B. Graves (1997) "The Corporate Social Performance–Financial Performance Link," *Strategic Management Journal* 18.4: 303-19.

Weiser, J., and S. Zadek (2000) *Conversations with Disbelievers. Persuading Companies to Address Social Challenges* (New York: The Ford Foundation).

Whetten, D.A., G. Rands, and P. Godfrey (2002) "What are the Responsibilities of Business to Society?" in A.M. Pettigrew, H. Thomas, and R. Whittington (eds.), *Handbook of Strategy and Management* (London: Sage): 373-409.

Wirtz, R.L. (1994) *Education and Training for the Baking Industry of the World: A History of the American Institute of Baking from Its Origins to the Present Day* (Manhattan, KS: Kansas State University).

Wood, D.J. (1991) "Corporate Social Performance Revisited," *Academy of Management Review* 16.4: 691-718.

WCED (World Commission on Environment and Development) (1987) *Our Common Future: Report of the World Commission on Environment and Development*, published as Annex to General Assembly document A/42/427; www.un-documents.net/wcedocf.htm, accessed January 29, 2009.

Wren, D.A. (1979) *The Evolution of Management Thought* (Hoboken, NJ: John Wiley).

Yates, J.D. (2007) "Creating a Hybrid: Collaboration between Not for Profit Organizations and For Profit Corporations," University of Oregon Scholar's Bank, https:// scholarsbank.uoregon.edu/dspace/handle/1794/5276, accessed January 29, 2009.

Appendix
List of hybrid organizations completing survey

Company name	HQ location				Environmental focus			Website
		Clean air	Clean water	Sustainable food/agriculture	Sustainable housing	Clean energy		
AbTech	U.S.A.		X					www.abtechindustries.com
Affirm–Aware	U.S.A.	X	X	X				www.affirm–aware.org
Annie's	U.S.A.			X				www.annies.com
BrightSource Energy	U.S.A.	X				X		www.brightsourceenergy.com
Burt's Bees	U.S.A.			X	X	X		www.burtsbees.com
Chemrec	Sweden					X		www.chemrec.se
CleanAir Logix	U.S.A.	X				X		www.cleanairlogix.com
CleanStar Energy	India			X		X		www.cleanstar.in
ClearFuels Technology, Inc.	U.S.A.	X		X		X		www.clearfuels.com
Clif Bar & Company	U.S.A.			X		X		www.clifbar.com
CoalTek	U.S.A.					X		www.coaltek.com
D.light design	U.S.A.					X		www.dlightdesign.com
Eden Foods	U.S.A.	X	X	X				www.edenfoods.com

Company name	HQ location	Environmental focus						Website
		Clean air	Clean water	Sustainable food/agriculture	Sustainable housing	Clean energy		
Electrocell Fuel Cells	Brazil		X		X	X		www.electrocell.com.br
EnerTech Environmental	U.S.A.					X		www.enertech.com
Freeplay Energy	UK					X		www.freeplayenergy.com
Greenline Industries	U.S.A.					X		www.greenlineindustries.com
Grille Zone restaurant	U.S.A.			X				www.grillezone.com
Guayakí Rainforest Products	U.S.A.			X	X			www.guayaki.com
H2Gen Innovations	U.S.A.					X		www.h2gen.com
Heritage Foods USA	U.S.A.	X	X	X				www.heritagefoodsusa.com
Ineeka	U.S.A.	X	X	X	X	X		www.ineeka.com
Intelligent Nutrients	U.S.A.			X				www.intelligentnutrients.com
JASCO Organics	U.S.A.	X	X					www.organicsbyjasco.com
Kona Blue Water Farms	U.S.A.			X				www.kona-blue.com
Magenn Power	Canada	X				X		www.magenn.com
Method Products	U.S.A.							www.methodhome.com
NanoH2O	U.S.A.		X					www.nanoh2o.com
Natura Cosméticos	Brazil	X	X	X		X		www.natura.net
New Belgium Brewing Co.	U.S.A.							www.newbelgium.com
Novazone	U.S.A.	X	X	X				www.novazone.com
PAX Scientific	U.S.A.	X	X			X		www.paxscientific.com
Picnick	U.S.A.			X				www.mypicnick.com
Purity	Sweden		X					www.purity.se

Company name	HQ location	Environmental focus						Website
		Clean air	Clean water	Sustainable food/agriculture	Sustainable housing	Clean energy		
PyroGenesis Canada	Canada	X	X				X	www.pyroGenesis.com
ReCellular	U.S.A.	X	X				X	www.recellular.com
Reforest Teak	U.S.A.	X	X	X	X		X	www.reforestteak.com
Seventh Generation	U.S.A.	X	X					www.seventhgeneration.com
SpringStar	U.S.A.			X				www.springstar.net
Stion	U.S.A.						X	www.stion.com
Stonyfield Farm	U.S.A.			X				www.stonyfield.com
SUN OVENS International	U.S.A.	X					X	www.sunoven.com
Targeted Growth	U.S.A.						X	www.targetedgrowth.com
Verdant Power	U.S.A.						X	www.verdantpower.com
Westport Innovations	Canada	X						www.westport.com
Zam–Bee–A Honey, Inc.	U.S.A.	X	X	X				www.zambezihoney.com
Ze–gen	U.S.A.		X					www.ze–gen.com

About the authors

Brewster Boyd began his career in management consulting with A.T. Kearney serving global corporate clients in the U.S. and Australia. He then worked with Ross & Associates Environmental Consulting in Seattle, a firm dedicated to helping public agencies improve management programs and achieve better environmental results. His work focuses on the development and financing of environmentally oriented technologies and businesses. He strives to contribute to organizations meeting basic human needs in a sustainable manner. He has an MBA and an MS through the University of Michigan's Erb Institute for Global Sustainable Enterprise and a BA from Middlebury College. Brewster lives with his family in Denver, Colorado.

Nina Henning is motivated by a desire to improve economic conditions in emerging markets through the development of business ventures that respect the environment and indigenous cultures. She has experience in financing the commercialization and distribution of clean technologies, both within the U.S. and internationally. In addition, Nina spent five years in Kathmandu, Nepal, as the Managing Director of Wild Earth Pvt. Ltd., a mission-driven herbal body-care company. Nina graduated from the University of Michigan's Erb Institute in 2009, earning an MBA from the Ross School of Business and an MS from the School of Natural Resources & Environment. She earned her BA in History from Princeton University.

Emily Reyna has a background in information technology: specifically, the field of Human Computer Interaction Design. She has held positions at Ford Motor Company, Apple Computer, Agilent Technologies, and SAP. While at Ford she became interested in corporate sustainability and started the Ford GreenIT Team. This work led her to the University of Michigan where she earned her MBA and an MS from the Erb Institute for Global Sustainable Enterprise. She is currently working for Environmental Defense Fund and its MBA Climate

Corps Program which embeds trained MBA students into corporations to identify energy efficiency improvements that can cut costs and reduce emissions. She holds a BS from Stanford University and currently lives in Southern California.

Daniel E. Wang enjoys helping organizations integrate environmental and social responsibility into their strategy and operational practice while ultimately driving change in consumer behavior at large. With eight years of engineering and management consulting experience, he has provided pro bono and fee-based services to public, private, and nonprofit sector clients across the world on a wide range of issues — from developing sustainability strategies for multinational corporations to writing business plans for national parks to facilitating funding opportunities for international development agencies. Dan holds an MBA and an MS from the University of Michigan's Erb Institute for Global Sustainable Enterprise and a BEng in Mechanical Engineering from McGill University. He currently works in Toronto, Canada, for Deloitte & Touche LLP in their Corporate Responsibility and Sustainability practice.

Matthew Welch has over ten years of experience in general management, sustainable development, and consulting with small businesses, nonprofit organizations, and *Fortune* 500 companies. He holds an MBA from the Ross School of Business and an MS in Natural Resources and Environment from the University of Michigan, and a BA in International Studies from DePaul University. Through his research and work experience he has gained a strong theoretical and practical knowledge of business and its effects on the social and environmental landscape. Matthew currently works for Dairy Management Inc. in Chicago focusing on strategy and stakeholder engagement for a wide-ranging sustainability initiative in the dairy industry.

Index

Page numbers in *italic figures* refer to figures and tables

Aché Guayakí people
Atlantic rainforest   69
Alter, Kim
hybrid spectrum   7–8, *8*
Apparel industry
Maggie's Organics   106–27
Assembly on location
GLOBAL SUN OVENS®   44, 47–8
Atlantic rainforest
Guayakí's commitment to   63, 64, 68, 69

B Corporation status
awarded to Guayakí   85
Becker, Sue   97–8, 101, 149
Bertone, Francesca   129, 131
Beverages
Guayakí's yerba mate   63–89
Biomass
reliance on, for cooking energy   38–9
Biomimicry
"innovation inspired by nature"   129–30, *130*
Bruehl, Richard   70, 72, 79, 84
Burda, Bená   110, 114–18, *116*, 119, 149
career turning point   *115*
leadership   107, 120–1
"Special Pioneer Award"   121
Burns, Tom   39, 52
Business models and strategies
Eden Foods   97–9, *97, 98*
Guayakí   71–6, *71, 74*, 86–7
hybrid organizations redefining   25–7, *26*
Maggie's Organics   112–19, *115, 116, 117*
mission and profit motivation   9, *9*
PAX Scientific   132–6, *132*
SUN OVENS   42–9, *45*, 57

Businesses
alliances with nonprofit organizations   15–17
limited success of traditional   7

Capitalism
promoting social and environmental missions   viii-x
Carbon credits
Guayakí's potential sale   87
Case studies
Eden Foods   90–105
Guayakí   63–89
Maggie's Organics   106–27
PAX Scientific   128–43
SUN OVENS International   37–62
Case study selection
hybrid organization survey   23–4
Cash flow
SUN OVENS' challenges   53
Ceremonial
traditional way to drink mate   66–7
Clean Clothes Inc.   119–20
Cleaning products
benefits of going green   vii-viii
Clothing industry
Maggie's Organics   106–27
Company study selection
hybrid organization survey   23–4
Competition
Eden Foods   93, 99
Guayakí   75–6
Maggie's Organics   119, 125, 127
premium products   148
solar ovens   49–51, *49*

Competitive advantage
sources of   27–8, *27*
Consumers
Guayakí's consumers   72, 88
Cooking
in developing countries   38–9
Corporate social responsibility (CSR)
linkages between social and financial
performance   12–14, *13*
Maggie's Organics   106–7, 121
Cost
related to competitive advantage   27–8, *28*
Cost structure
SUN OVENS' model   54–5, *55*
Cotton growing
conventional/organic   106, 109–10

Data-gathering methodology
research into hybrid organizations   18–24
Deforestation
in Haiti   56
reliance on biomass fuel   38–9
Design
GLOBAL SUN OVEN®   *41*, 44, 578
Design geometries
inspired by biomimicry   129–30, 141
Developed-country markets
SUN OVENS   43, *45*
SUN OVENS' market risks   60–1
Developing-country markets
SUN OVENS   43–4, *45*
Distribution
Guayakí's yerba mate   72–3
Maggie's Organics   118–19, 125, 149

Eco-friendly packaging   86–7
Economic viability
see Financial viability
Eden Foods
business strategy and model   97–9, *97, 98*
challenges for the future   105
goals and objectives   94, *94*
liabilities and obligations   100, *100*
organic industry acquisitions   *92*
overview and history   91–7, *91*
Engineering research and development
PAX Scientific   128–43
Entrepreneurship
see Sustainable entrepreneurship
Environmental benefits
change from biomass to solar
power   38–9
Environmental features
competitive advantage   27–8, *27*
Environmental metrics tracking
Eden Foods   103

Guayakí   83–5
hybrid organization survey   34–5, *34*
Maggie's Organics   122–3
PAX Scientific   140–1
SUN OVENS   56–7
Environmental mission
embedded in hybrids' business
model   144–5
Environmental outcomes
PAX Water Technologies   135
Environmental responsibility
household cleaners   vii-viii
Maggie's Organics   106–7, 121
Environmental stewardship
combined with financial viability   6
Guayakí   74
Environmental sustainability
case study selection criteria   20, *20*
criteria   10
criteria for mission-driven companies   10
Eden Foods' focus on sustainability   103
Guayakí's commitment to   85, 149
impact of hybrid organizations   6
integration throughout organization   33–
5, *33*
PAX Scientific   140
PAX Water   140

Fair Trade Zone (FTZ) Sewing Co-
operative   114, 116–18, *117*
Finance
Eden Foods   99–100
Guayakí   76–9
Maggie's Organics   119–20
PAX Scientific   136–8, *137*
SUN OVENS   51–4, *52*
Financial performances
linkages with corporate social
responsibility   12–14, *13*
Financial risk
SUN OVENS' outlook   62
Financial viability
combined with environmental
stewardship   6
Guayakí   75
hybrid organization survey   28–9, *28*, 36
Financing sources
advantage or challenge seen in   30–1, *30*
hybrid organization survey   29–30, *29*, 36
Fluid-handling equipment
PAX Scientific   128–43
Food products
Eden Foods   90–105
For-profit/nonprofit spectrum   7
social enterprise in the context of   15–17

FTZ
   see Fair Trade Zone (FTZ) Sewing Co-
      operative
Fuel
   reliance on biomass   38–9

"Green" products
   competitive advantage   27–8, *27*
Growth
   managing the rate of growth   147–8
Guayakí
   challenges for the future   87–8
   company background   67–9
   goals and objectives   70
   headquarters relocation   76
   introduction and overview   63–71
   managing rate of growth   147–8
   ownership structure   77–8
   Paraguay project   69
   supply chain   69
Guayakí Rainforest Preserve   68–9

Harman, Jay   128–32
   "serial entrepreneur"   131
Hawken, Paul   134
Health benefits
   cooking with solar ovens   38–9
   organic yerba mate   63, 64, 65, 68, 71–2
Health threats
   pesticides used on cotton   109
HIV/AIDS
   impact of SUN OVENS in South Africa   56
Hybrid organizations
   business practices   3, 144–9, *151*
   criteria for selection   18–20, *20*
   definitions   5–10, 151
   demographics of survey
      respondents   21–2, *22*
   effectiveness revisited   152–3
   key trends   *2*
   practices   3
   research literature   11–17
   survey analysis   21–2, *22*
   survey data   2, 3
   trends and lessons from survey   25–36, *26*
   see also Case studies
Hybrid ovens
   discontinued by SUN OVENS   49–50
Hybrid spectrum   7–8, *8*

Innovation
   Eden Foods   104
   Guayakí   86–7
   hybrids reporting "notable
      innovations"   35–6, *35*
   Maggie's Organics   124–5

PAX's biomimicry design for fluid
      propulsion   129–30, 141
SUN OVENS   57–9
Innovative product features
   competitive advantage   27–8, *27*
Interviews
   hybrid organization survey   24

Japan
   food products imported into U.S.   93

Karr, David   67–8
Karr, Steve   68
Khosla Ventures   136, 137–8

Leadership
   Eden Foods   90–1, 101
   Guayakí   79
   Maggie's Organics   107, 120–1
   PAX Scientific   131–2
   SUN OVENS   54, 62
Leadership styles
   hybrid organization survey   32, *32*
   patience and morality of Paul
      Munsen   38
Legal structure
   Eden Foods   102
   Maggie's Organics   121
   SUN OVENS   55
Macrobiotics
   background to Eden Foods   93
Maggie's Organics
   challenges for the future   125–6
   goals and objectives   111
   overview and history   106–12, *107*
   relationship with FTZ   116–18, *117*
   sourcing   113, 121
Mann, Chris   63, 68, 72
Market premium products
   rare price advantage   148
Market redefinition
   by hybrid organizations   25–7, *26*
Market risk
   Eden Foods   105
   Maggie's organics   125–7
   SUN OVENS   60–1
Market-driven restoration
   Guayakí's commitment to Atlantic
      Forest   64, 70, 74, *74*
Markets
   Eden Foods   97–8, 99
   Guayakí's yerba mate   71–3, 147
   PAX Scientific   132–3, 147
   PAX Water Technologies   135
   SUN OVENS' marketing on location   44, 46–8
   SUN OVENS' strategic positioning   42–4, *42*

Mate   viii, ix, 36, 145, 147
    cultivation and processing   66
    product description   63, 65, 70–1, 86
    sourced in Atlantic rainforest   68–9
    traditional way to drink   66–7
Methodology
    research into hybrid organizations   18–24
Metrics
    see Environmental metrics tracking
Microfinance
    combined with product promotion   58
Mission and culture
    Eden Foods   *91*, 101–2, 145
    Guayakí   80–3, 88, 145
    Maggie's Organics   107, 111, 120–2, 145
    PAX Scientific   139–40, 142–3
    SUN OVENS   55, 145
Mission implementation
    hybrid organizations   144–5
Mission objectives
    SUN OVENS' risk awareness   58–9
Mission statement
    Guayakí   *64*
    SUN OVENS International, Inc.   *38*
Mixing technology
    PAX Mixer   135–6
Motivation
    see Organizational motivation
Mueller, Jennifer   110, 119
Munsen, Paul   39, 44, 47, 49–56, 62
Murray, Peter   114

Newton, Michael   68
NGOs (non-governmental organizations)
    SUN OVENS' NGO model   48–9
Nicaragua
    community sustainability   116
    Nueva Vida co-operative   107, 114, 116–18
Non-governmental organizations
    see NGOs
Nonprofit organizations
    alliances with businesses   15–17
    need for social enterprise models   6–7
Nonprofit/for-profit spectrum   7
    social enterprise in the context of   15–17
Nueva Vida co-operative   107, 114, 116–18

Organic cotton
    accreditation   110, 111, 121
    contrasted with conventional   109–10
Organic cotton apparel
    industry overview   108–9
Organic fibers
    certifying organizations   110

Organic products
    Eden Foods   90–105
    Guayakí's yerba mate   63–89
Organizational motivation
    financial viability with environmental stewardship   6
    mission and profit dimensions   9, *9*
Organizational risk
    Eden Foods   105
    Maggie's organics   125–7
    SUN OVENS' leadership   62
Organizational structure
    Eden Foods   101–3
    Guayakí   79–83, *81*, *82*
    Maggie's Organics   120–2
    PAX Scientific   138–40, *139*
    SUN OVENS   54–6
Ovens
    solar   37–62

Packaging
    Guayakí's tea bags   86–7
Parabolic solar ovens   *49*, 50
Patagonia
    organic cotton   108–9
Patience
    required by stakeholders   147
Patient capital sources
    financing hybrid organizations   29–30, *29*, 36
PAX Mixer   135–6
PAX Scientific
    challenges for the future   141–3
    licensee companies   133–6
    overview and history   129–30
    relationship with shareholders   146
PAX Streamline   136, 137–9
PAX Streamlining Principle   130
PaxAuto   134
PaxFan   134–5
PaxIT   134
Personal relationships
    see Relationships
Pesticides
    on conventionally grown cotton   109
Potter, Michael   90–1, 95, 101
Price
    premium products   148
Private voluntary organizations
    see PVOs
Problems
    see World problems
Product development
    Eden Foods   104
Product information
    Eden Foods   94–7, *96*

GLOBAL SUN OVEN 39, 40–1, *41*
Guayakí 63, 64, 65, 70–1
Maggie's Organics 111–12
SUN OVENS International 40–2, *41*
VILLAGER SUN OVEN® 40, 44
Product promotion
combined with microfinance 58
Production
Maggie's Organics 113–18, 121
Profit motivation
for-profit/nonprofit spectrum 7, 15–17
mission and profit dimensions 9, *9*
Profitability margins
hybrid organization survey 28–9, *28*, 36
Pryor, Alex 67–8
PVOs (private voluntary organizations)
SUN OVENS' working relationship
with 48–9

Quality
related to competitive advantage 27–8, *27*
Quality control
Eden Foods 99, 148–9
Maggie's Organics 126–7

Rainforests
Guayakí's restorative business
model 63, 64, 68–9, 73–5
Reforestation
South American Atlantic Forest 64, 74
Relationships
Maggie's Organics 146
success stemming from 146
SUN OVENS 146
Research
into hybrid organizations 11–17
Research methodology
research into hybrid organizations 18–24
Respondents
hybrid organization survey 21–2, *22*
Restoration, market driven
see Market-driven restoration
Retail sales
Maggie's Organics *108*, 110–11, 118–19
Risk
SUN OVENS' multiple business risks 58–62
see also Market risk; Organizational risk;
Financial risk
Ritual
traditional way to drink mate 66–7
Rotary International
and SUN OVENS 39, 42, 49

Sales
Maggie's Organics *108*, 110–11, 118–19

Sampling
for hybrid company selection 18–20, *20*
Seventh Generation vii, viii, 147
Social enterprise and business
nonprofit alliances 15–17
Social and environmental issues
reluctance of businesses to address 7
Social justice
Guayakí 74–5
Social responsibility
see Corporate social responsibility
Solar ovens
case study 37–62
low-technology versions 50
Solomon, Jon 103
South America
Guayakí's rainforest-grown mate 63, 64,
68–9
Standards
organic cotton accreditation 110, 111,
121
Strategies
see Business models and strategies
Succession planning
Eden Foods 90–1
SUN OVENS International
goals and objectives 40
managing rate of growth 148
overview and history 37–9, *38*
product promotion with
microfinance 58
Suppliers
Eden Foods working with 93, 94–5, 98–9,
104, 146
Survey analysis
research into hybrid organizations 21–2,
22
Sustainability
see Environmental sustainability
Sustainable entrepreneurship 11
recent research 14–15
Swaney, Bill 101, 103

Triple-bottom-line approach
Guayakí's business model 64, 72, 74–5,
85, 86
SUN OVENS 148

United Nations Millennium Goals
most challenging world problems 6

Venture capitalists x, 78, 137, 142
Venture financing
PAX Scientific with Khosla Ventures 137–8
Viability
see Financial viability

Virtue Ventures 6–7
Vortices
  design geometries inspired by
        biomimicry 129–30, 131

Wages
  Guayakí defining a living wage 87
  Maggie's Organics 122
Water mixers
  PAX Water Technologies 135
Wholesale sales
  Maggie's Organics 118

Whole-grain foods
  background to Eden Foods 93
Wilson, Doug 112
Woodard, Michael 114, *116*, 117–18
World problems
  requiring large-scale solutions 6–8

Yerba mate
  see Mate